Praise for *A S*

"When you're reading Neal's work, especia
you find yourself afraid to read more — b
reading. There's no question that Neal's work is uniquely memorable and his
'book of secrets' should be a must-read for anyone interested in writing in the
genre." **—Joel Roodman**, founder of Gotham Entertainment Group, former senior
executive with Miramax Films

"Stevens has mastered that ability to know and understand what makes us all
afraid, and has the ability to apply that knowledge in his writing." **—Jim Strader**,
Co-Creator of *Weird America*, and CEO and Publisher at Quattro Media

"No script ever magically appears. It is the work, the toil, the sweat and blood
of a master, a professional, who understands the craft of manipulation through
thoughtfully, yet spontaneously, telling a well-constructed story ... a story that
will make you scream in terror, yet drive you to laughter within a few lines
of exposition. A story that makes you want to throw a book or script across
a room out of fear — but you can't, because you *must* find out what will happen next. And THAT is what *A Sense of Dread* is about. You will love this
book."**—Michael Citriniti**, Actor, *Goodfellas, Ravenwolf Towers*

"There are a lot of ingredients in putting together a successful horror story or film.
But I'm delighted to say that author Neal Marshall Stevens has put those compo-
nents together in *A Sense of Dread: Getting Under the Skin of Horror Screenwriting*!
Stevens boldly tackles the subject of "fear" by providing writers with ways to take
their characters (and all of us) on a terror-filled, but informational journey, on crafting a horror project! Read it, if you dare!!!"**—Kathie Fong Yoneda**, Former Studio
Exec, Author of *The Script-Selling Game*

"*A Sense of Dread* doesn't just demonstrate how to write a horror script — it's a
primer in how our minds work (often against us) and a history of fear and terror
throughout the ages. *A Sense of Dread* shows us that our biggest fears don't just
come from monsters, demons, or spirits — but our very humanity: fragile, vulnerable, irrational. It is rich, fast-paced, and eminently readable.
"*A Sense of Dread* is a must-read — not only for horror writers, but all writers, or
anyone interested in the fascinating background behind our fears, phobias, and
what makes us uniquely human." **—Matthew Reynolds**, Hollywood Executive,
who developed the screenplays for *Hidalgo, Ladder 49*, and the Netflix hit
The Highwaymen

"In *A Sense of Dread*, Neal Marshall Stevens expertly gets to the heart of the scare. What makes us afraid and how you can turn those fears into a career!" **—Tony Timpone**, Former Editor of *Fangoria Magazine*, Producer and Author

"Literally littered with horrific ideas ... and that's a good thing. No matter your experience in the horror genre, *A Sense of Dread* will flood you with ideas for scenes, characters, and stories. Neal stares deep into the heart of what makes us afraid without making us, the reader, afraid. He unpacks our Sense of Dread at the most primal, biological, and psychological level. However, the text is light and easy to read, making a dip into the swamp of the horrific feel like a refreshing dip in a tidal pool." **—Matthew Kalil**, Author of *The Three Wells of Screenwriting*, Professor at the David Lynch Graduate School of Cinematic Arts MFA in Screenwriting Program

"Neal Stevens' love for — and encyclopedic knowledge of — the horror genre is obvious to everyone who knows him. In *A Sense of Dread,* he shares his profound understanding of the psychology of fear, from our terrified responses to creepy critters to our deepest personal and social anxieties, then gives budding horror writers the tools they need to use that knowledge and master their craft. Read this book if you hope to overcome any fear you might have of turning out a truly terrifying script!" **—Dorothy Rompalske**, Filmmaker, Writer, and Director/ Chair of the David Lynch Graduate School of Cinematic Arts MFA Program in Screenwriting

"Anyone interested in the craft of horror screenwriting should definitely take a look at his 'book of secrets.'" **—Denice Duff**, Actor, best known to horror fans for her role in the *Subspecies* series of films

"*A Sense of Dread* deftly manages to be both concise and comprehensive. An absorbing read that touches all bases, making it a must-have for both fans and creators." **—F. Paul Wilson**, best-selling Author of science fiction and horror, including the *Repairman Jack* novels

"In working with Neal Stevens, I discovered the extent of Neal's dark imagination and his broad knowledge of the horror genre, a deep well of sinister knowledge that he's now decided to share in his book, *A Sense of Dread: Getting Under the Skin of Horror Screenwriting.*

"Neal has managed to incorporate a vast amount of experience in crafting a work that digs down into the fundamentals of fear and also details its practical application on both the page and the screen. It's a must-read for any writer interested in the horror genre." **—Gil Adler**, Producer, Writer, Director, his work includes *Tales from the Crypt*, *Thirteen Ghosts*, and *Superman Returns* among others.

A SENSE OF
DREAD

GETTING UNDER THE SKIN OF HORROR SCREENWRITING

NEAL MARSHALL STEVENS

MICHAEL WIESE PRODUCTIONS

Published by Michael Wiese Productions
12400 Ventura Blvd. #1111
Studio City, CA 91604
(818) 379-8799, (818) 986-3408 (Fax)
mw@mwp.com
www.mwp.com
Manufactured in the
United States of America

This book was set in Garamond Premier Pro and Din Pro

Cover design by Johnny Ink
Interior design by Debbie Berne
Copyediting by Sarah Beach

Names: Stevens, Neal Marshall, author.
Title: A sense of dread: getting under the skin of horror screenwriting / Neal Stevens.
Description: Studio City: Michael Wiese Productions, [2022] | Identifiers: LCCN 2021013988 | ISBN 9781615933334 (trade paperback)
Subjects: LCSH: Horror films—Authorship. | Motion picture plays—Technique. | Motion picture authorship. | Fear.
Classification: LCC PN1995.9.H6 S748 2022 | DDC 808.2/3—dc23

LC record available at https://lccn.loc.gov/2021013988

To Judith, Jacob, and Zachary

CONTENTS

I started working with Neal over two decades ago, and the movie business has been through lots of changes over that time. What hasn't changed is our mutual love of movies, monsters, and horror — and the joy of bringing that special combination of scares, thrills, and just plain weirdness to our audiences.

Neal has a deep (might I say almost scary?) knowledge of horror movies — old Universal classics, Euro-horror, obscure low-budget creepy rarities from the fifties and sixties. If I mention some rare horror flick as a reference for something we're developing, chances are he's not only seen it, but probably already owns a copy.

Over our years together, Neal has worked on everything from our own unique take on giant monster movies — *Zarkorr! The Invader* and *Kraa the Sea Monster* to children's fantasy — *The Shrunken City, Clockmaker,* and *The Secret Kingdom,* to our own unique combination of horror and off-beat comedy with movies such as *Head of the Family, Hideous,* and *The Creeps!* to straight horror in projects like *Talisman, Stitches* (which he directed) and his multiple contributions to our perennial *Puppetmaster* series.

More recently, he's gone on to contribute his talents to our streaming projects — *Trophy Heads* and *Ravenwolf Towers.*

Neal's originality, talent, and just plain oddball sensibility as a screenwriter has made him an invaluable contributor to the crazy, scary, and definitely weird Full Moon Family!

So, read on!

—*Charles Band*

Charles Band has been the first name in low-budget, high-concept genre entertainment for over forty years. For more about him check out the information on page XXX.

INTRODUCTION

I heard a slight groan, and I knew it was the groan of mortal terror.
Edgar Allan Poe

Tales of Horror have been with us since before the beginnings of history. From time immemorial, they have been whispered around the campfire, painted on the walls of caves, and passed down in song, story, and myth. We have gone in search of the things that terrify us, maybe to learn from them, maybe to test ourselves, maybe for some reason we don't quite understand.

Our most ancient narratives that come down to us from before the beginning of recorded history speak of the confrontation of our ancestors with their darkest fears.

But what, after all, is horror? What horrifies us and why? Is it simply the fear of what lurks unseen in the dark, or the fear of death, or of physical injury?

Then there's the larger question: What is it that tempts us to experience horror, whether in the spoken word, on the page, on the stage, on the screen? What is that urge that makes us want to peer through our fingers at those forbidden and often subversive images on the screen?

What is it that draws so many of us to those sharp edges of experience and imagination?

That is part of what we are going to explore in this book — the nature of fear itself; where it comes from, what fears we have in common with other members of the animal kingdom, what fears are uniquely human, what fears are tied to particular times, cultures, and places.

We will also explore whether fear and horror are the same thing, and if they differ, what distinguishes one from the other?

I believe that the emotion of horror is embodied in what I call the *Sense of Dread*.

Here are some examples:

In Robert Wise's *The Haunting* (1963) — when the unseen force that haunts Hill House approaches Eleanor and Dorothea's room in the form of a terrifying banging in the hallway outside — and then jiggles the doorknob, trying to get in.

In Stanley Kubrick's *The Shining* (1980) — when Wendy finds the unattended typewriter containing the "novel" that Jack's been working on for endless weeks — only to discover that page after page consists of nothing but "All work and no play makes Jack a dull boy. . . ."

In James Wan's *The Conjuring* (2013) — when the terrified daughter stares into the darkness behind her half-open bedroom door and whispers to her sister, "There's someone behind the door."

What's important to note is that in none of these examples is there any immediate physical danger. To the extent that there may be a physical threat, it is indefinite, lurking elsewhere, beyond a door, or unseen in the shadows.

Dread runs deeper than simply the apprehension of physical danger. It's the difference between facing a lion in the jungle as opposed to hearing the scratch of claws behind the wall. It's the difference between being confronted by a man with a gun as opposed to discovering a worm crawling under your skin.

We experience the *Sense of Dread* when that which we believe to be safe, secure, or sacred is unexpectedly penetrated or violated by The Forbidden, The Unknown, or The Unnatural.

In the Chapters that follow, we will explore both Fear and its origins and also the concept of Dread.

We'll try to learn how we, as screenwriters, can understand and use them.

1

FEAR ITSELF, PART ONE
THE BIOLOGICAL BASIS OF FEAR

The only thing we have to fear is — fear itself.
Franklin Delano Roosevelt (1933)

Biology lies at the base of our fundamental experiences of fear.

The emotion of fear is linked with what is commonly known as the fight/flight reflex, a response that we share with virtually every member of the animal kingdom with a working brain above a certain level of complexity.

The structure known as the amygdala, located near the brain stem, regulates fear in human beings (it serves many other functions as well). It's one of the most primitive parts of the brain, and is found in all mammals, from shrews to the blue whale. While it may enter into the realms of speculation, other members of the animal kingdom, from reptiles to amphibians to fish, might also experience the emotion of fear.

However, that doesn't mean that, even for human beings, the experience of fear is universal. Sufferers from an extremely rare genetic disorder known as Urbach-Wiethe disease, which can lead to lesions forming on the amygdala, can sometimes exhibit a complete lack of the emotion of fear.

Here's a particularly grim example from another species. For the mouse, their experience of fear, under normal circumstances, usually keeps them lurking safely in corners. But they undergo a strange change of behavior when infected by the toxoplasma parasite.

The mouse is only one stop on the parasite's intricate reproductive journey. Inside the mouse, the parasite travels to the brain, where it causes the mouse to lose its fear of cat odor — bad for the mouse but good for the parasite that infects it, and that's because a fearless mouse tends to stray out into the open, where it is apt to be eaten by a cat. Inside the cat's gut, the parasite is able to complete its reproductive cycle.

As a side note, one study found an increased level of traffic accidents among human beings infected with the toxoplasma parasite. If thinking about this is starting to creep you out — well, at least it suggests that your amygdala is present and working well.

But the above raises a more profound question. Just how far does it go? What aspects of our own fears can we recognize and understand in other animals?

I'd like to talk about a number of fears that we share with other members of the Animal Kingdom.

• • •

Temple Grandin is well-known as an animal scientist who has used her unique insights born from her autism to investigate the internal lives and thought processes of other living creatures. In her book *Animals in Translation* (2005), written with Catherine Johnson, she discusses some of the fear responses that we share with other animals.

These are some of her conclusions.

FEAR OF THE UNKNOWN IS UNIVERSAL

It's as true for a cow, a cat, or a dog, as it is for us. But matters are more complicated than that. We all live in a world that is full of new experiences. Full of "unknowns." If we simply ran away from everything new, we wouldn't survive for long. On the other hand, if we blundered around, failing to take proper precautions around the new and strange, we'd likely end up on the inside of — well, something new, strange — and deadly.

Grandin talks about the behavior of cattle, noting that they're easily spooked, that they'll run from anything novel in their environment. But they're also very curious animals. They have to be, because it's only by investigating their environment that they can find food, avoid danger, and maintain social relationships.

CURIOUSLY AFRAID

So what happens when you introduce some novel object into a field where cattle are grazing? Well, if it's something new and moving toward them, there's no question what to do. They get out. Fast.

But what if it isn't approaching them?

Then they exhibit a behavior that Grandin refers to as being *curiously afraid*. This is a behavior that's broadly exhibited across the Animal Kingdom and should be very familiar to anyone who's ever watched a horror movie.

This is how it works for cattle. If something new enters the environment and is obviously dangerous, there's no question as to what to do. They'll run. If something enters the environment and is obviously familiar and of no use to them (that is, it's not food or a potential mate), there's also no question as to how to behave. They ignore it and go on about their business.

But what if it's ambiguous? Something they're just not sure

about. Maybe it's nothing — or maybe it's dangerous. Maybe it's useful; something good to eat, for instance. Just leaving it alone isn't a good idea. Whether you're a cow, a cat, or a human being, you need to find out.

Thus you find yourself in the midst of that competing tension of emotion that Grandin calls being "curiously afraid."

In the case of the cattle, they will very cautiously approach the novel object, extend their heads, their tongues, examining "whatever-it-is." Touch, taste, wait to see if there's any sign of danger. If so, if they're startled, then they'll get the hell out of there. If not, and having investigated fully and come to the conclusion that whatever-it-is is neither useful nor harmful, they'll go back to doing what they do best. Eating grass.

But what's the human equivalent? Where have we seen examples of human beings being "curiously afraid"?

How many times have we watched that scene in a horror movie of someone walking down the long corridor toward the half-open door? Or down the dimly-lit cluttered alley way? Or down the basement stairs where they've heard a sound and where the lights are now no longer working?

There is no explicit visual danger. If there were, they'd get the hell out of there. No, the menace is always ambiguous. Its nature is such that, even though we're always saying, "don't do it, get the hell out of there," at the same time we know that they really can't.

We, like the characters in those horror movies, are curiously afraid. Even though we suspect that something terrible is likely lurking behind the half open door or down at the bottom of those dimly lit basement steps — still, curiosity drives both them and us.

Both of us have to go on, to find out. Maybe it's nothing.

Only of course, in the real world, that may be true. But in a horror movie, on some level we know that ultimately, there will always be something there, lurking in the shadows.

THE STARTLE RESPONSE

This is something else that we share with other members of the animal kingdom. Pretty much anybody who's owned a cat knows what happens if you sneak up on it and poke it with your finger (which I used to do to our rather high-strung pet, back when I was an ill-behaved kid growing up in Boston).

Needless to say, a startled cat can jump really high.

The same is true with virtually any mammal, including us. A sudden unexpected touch, sound, appearance, will produce the traditional "startle" response. We'll jump, gasp, blink, pull back. Our hearts will beat faster.

The sudden intrusion has triggered the flow of adrenalin. It's triggered our "fight or flight" response. Essentially, we have a built-in alarm system that's not particularly discriminating. All that it does is react to something close that we didn't expect and don't immediately recognize.

The biological alarm instantly goes off!

Get ready to fight! Get ready to run! As with many such indiscriminate alarm systems, it's set far toward the "false positive" side. Much better, when it comes to preserving our lives, to jump every so often over nothing, than to not be startled when you should and end up inside the stomach of a sabre-tooth tiger.

Anyone who's ever watched a horror movie knows that filmmakers have taken advantage of the startle response since the beginning of motion pictures. The advent of sound increased the effectiveness of the startle response, which these days is called a "Jump scare" or a "boo."

In contemporary movies, it's rare for us to see a jump scare of any kind without it being amplified on the sound track with some sort of loud orchestral *blare* to send us jumping out of our seats.

Of course, since this is a biological response, the reaction isn't limited to horror movies. There are any number of thrillers, suspense films, and action films that make use of the startle response to get the audience to jump out of their seats. Bodies drop out of closets. Hands reach in from just out of frame. Telephones suddenly — RINNNNGG!!! — at a much louder volume than reason dictates.

And, of course, it always works, because those moments bypass reason, and go straight to our most ancient biological reflexes.

. . .

In a later chapter, we'll go into greater detail about the uses of the "curiously afraid" reaction and the startle response — the countless variations that have been used in movies down through the years, and how modern screenwriters can make use of them in crafting their own new scary scenes and sequences.

FEAR AND THE MAPPING OF THE BRAIN

As we know intuitively, the vast network of our body's nervous system doesn't treat every part of our body equally. Some parts of our bodies receive the lion's share of both sensory nerves and pain receptors. Some of us may remember an old summer camp game where someone draws a number with the tip of a finger on someone else's back. Can you guess the number? It's harder than you think, simply because the back, compared for instance, to the palm of the hand, is sparsely equipped with sensory nerves.

It's equally true that certain parts of our body are much more sensitive to pain than others.

In 1937, Doctors Wilder Penfield, Edwin Boldrey and Theodore Rasmussen, conducting investigations of human brain function, created what they called sensory and motor "homunculi;" that is, they created physical representations of the human body based on how much of the brain was devoted to a given portion of the human anatomy.

Many years later, this three-dimensional sculpture of the "sensory homunculus" was created, based on their initial research:

Apart from looking like something out of a horror movie, what is intriguing about the above image is that it bears a striking similarity to drawings of the human form made by very young children.

Take this example, for instance:

What do we see emphasized? Head, mouth, eyes, nose, hands. In the drawings of young children, the torsos are often literally absent, with limbs simply grafted onto the head.

This is telling us something about the way in which children develop — which is that they "see" people not as we are physically, not as their eyes perceive us, but as their brains perceive themselves.

Mostly, as we grow older, our mental map of ourselves tracks with greater precision to our objective physical form. But sometimes, there can be a pathological mismatch, as in the case of sufferers from anorexia, who, even when underweight to the point of near-starvation, will look at themselves and "see" someone who is overweight. Or in the case of those unfortunate individuals who suffer from "phantom limb" syndrome, they continue to feel pain in arms or legs that have been amputated.

But what does all of this have to do with horror movies or with the Sense of Dread?

Quite simply this: When we talk about those biologically-based aspects of fear, we have to go back to that "sensory homunculus," to those aspects of the human body that are most sensitive, most heavily "wired" to feel pain.

From our earliest childhood, we instinctively react with horror to the prospect of injury to certain parts of our bodies. Specifically, injury to the extremities:

Hands, Fingers, Wrists, Feet, Toes, Ankles

And the front of the face:

Eyes, Nose, Lips, Tongue, Teeth

And getting our *Hair* tangled or pulled out.

Here are some classic examples:

- Jack Nicholson's nose being slit open in Roman Polanski's *Chinatown* (1974)
- Jon Voight's crushed fingertip from Andrei Konchalovsky's *Runaway Train* (1985)
- Richard Burton's spike-pierced foot from John Boorman's *Exorcist Part II* (1977)
- James Caan has his ankles broken in Rob Reiner's *Misery* (1990)
- Peter Cushing has his hand chopped off in Terence Fisher's *Island of Terror* (1966)
- The unfortunate woman's eye pierced by a splinter in Lucio Fulci's *Zombie* (1979)
- Dustin Hoffman's dental torture scene from John Schlesinger's *Marathon Man* (1976)

There are many other examples and I leave it to you to think of your own.

Of course, *Chinatown, Runaway Train*, and *Marathon Man* aren't horror movies, and yet we often find, not only in these movies but in countless other examples, that so-called mainstream cinema turns to the tropes of horror cinema for some of their most effective and memorable images, scenes, and sequences.

EXERCISES ·

- Come up with a list from movies you've seen of effective examples of Jump Scares.
- Come up with another list of effective "curiously afraid" moments.

- Come up with another list of effective moments or scenes from movies (horror movies or otherwise), that took advantage of "brain mapping" sensitivity by targeting eyes, fingers, extremities, etc.

In the next chapter, we'll continue to explore the ways in which the nature of fear connects not only to human biology, but also to that which makes us uniquely human, to human psychology, and to our place in a changing society.

2

PSYCHOLOGICALLY-BASED FEARS

Presently I heard a slight groan, and I knew
it was the groan of mortal terror.

Edgar Allen Poe

INSTINCTIVE FEARS

Many years ago philosophers believed in the so-called "tabula rasa," that we were born as "blank slates" on which our parents, society, or the experiences of our up-bringing inscribed our personalities, our loves, our fears, our preferences, needs, cravings, and desires.

Scientific research (and the accumulated insight of countless parents and caregivers) have led us to understand that we are far more complicated beings than the mere sum of our experiences. That just as many of the fellow organisms with which we share this planet come into the world equipped with instinctive behaviors as well as the ability to learn from experience, the human "slate" with which we are born is far from blank.

Research into young children indicates that certain fears are, if not universal, at the very least, broadly shared among young children in widely diverse cultures, circumstances, and up-bringing.

Fear of Rats, Mice, and Other Scurrying Things

This is a fear that arises very early in childhood. It is the especial tendency of rodents to occupy the corners and crevices of our own living spaces that seems to intensify the sense of loathing that we have for them. And while there are always exceptions to any rule, it appears clear that the sense of horror, the Dread of the Rodent is something that runs deep into our DNA — a loathing that we seem to share with other mammals.

It's important to understand that this fear of rodents isn't inherently rational. A rat, for instance, isn't any more dangerous, say, than a fox. In fact, a fox is certainly more dangerous. But the prospect of finding a fox in your bedroom may be surprising and even scary, but it wouldn't fill you with the sense of sheer loathing, that "Sense of Dread," that you would feel at discovering a rat in your bedroom.

Why? Because the fear of foxes is learned. We have to learn that foxes are dangerous by observing their appearance and behavior (or learning through others). The horror of rats is built in. Our reaction to them is instant and visceral.

One should note that our fear of rodents extends to bats. Though they're not officially members of the rodent family, in appearance and behavior, our instinctive reactions tend to group them together, we think of them as flying mice or even worse — flying rats.

Fear of Spiders

This is another widely experienced instinctive fear.

Now, the Arthropoda covers a wide range of species and genera; the spiders, the insects, the millipedes — countless crawly, biting, stinging things in sea and air — so our reactions to the whole range of things that fly and buzz and crawl and bite and sting like-wise covers a broad range.

Not many people are terrified by butterflies or caterpillars, nor even by mosquitoes despite the fact that over the centuries the diseases that mosquitoes have carried have probably been responsible for more human deaths than all the wars combined. But we simply think of them as an annoyance; we don't dread them. We're not horrified by a mosquito bite.

On the other hand, *spiders* in particular, trigger that instinctive reaction of dread in a way that bumblebees or dragonflies do not (not that there aren't people who are afraid of those insects as well).

Fear of Snakes
We've saved the scariest for last. Here, as a sub-category of the fear of reptiles, we find the single greatest fear among both children and adults. 51% of Americans surveyed reported snakes as their number one fear. This is true even among those who have grown up with essentially no direct experience of snakes.

Fear of Choking, Smothering, or Drowning
The above group is, likewise, one of those common, instinctive fears. We don't need to look very deeply for the reason for this one, of course. If our brains are deprived of life-giving oxygen for three minutes, we'll die. Not being able to breathe almost immediately triggers a biological reaction, that desperate sense of smothering, usually coupled with panic, the fight-or-flight response. It's a tragic irony that this panic response often overwhelms the ability of someone who finds themselves choking or drowning to make decisions that might actually save their lives.

While the fear of choking or drowning seems self-evident, what about the others? Where do they come from, these fears of rats, of spiders, of snakes? Surely the world is full of many things that are far more dangerous. For instance, young children have no fear of those chemical poisons that lurk in bottles beneath the sink. However dangerous they are, there's no instinctive aversion to deadly chemicals, no natural protective safety valve that makes us fear or avoid them. We simply have to learn to stay away from them.

It's pretty clear that these deeper fears aren't learned. That is, they don't come from outside of us. The fear doesn't come from the rats, or the spiders, or the snakes themselves. These fears come from within. They are genetically programmed by the forces of natural selection, for reasons that reach back into the dim mists of our ancient human or perhaps even pre-human ancestry.

Again, we go back to that fight-or-flight reflex and to the instincts that trigger it, the potentially dangerous things that creep and crawl in the underbrush beneath our feet and in the corners and in the shadows. It would have been lethal for our ancient ancestors to wait long enough to find out just what it was that was doing the scratching or the crawling or the scurrying.

Instinct had to take over, to send the adrenalin pumping and to hit that internal button that makes our skin crawl and every sense react with an instinctive loathing and trigger the urge to jump back, retreat, lash out and get the hell away from those scratching, scurrying nightmares in the shadow.

CROSS-OVER FEARS

Some of our fears are unquestionably built-in. Others are most definitely learned. For instance, we seem to have no instinctive *fear of fire* despite the fact that it's very definitely dangerous. The human race just seems to have met up with it in the mists of pre-history too late for us to have developed any instincts about it. We have to put our fingers into the flames a few times before we start being afraid of it. It is a "learned" fear. We'll talk about learned fears shortly.

But there is another category of fears, an intermediate category of things that are feared by a great many people that, for lack of a better way of thinking about it, may have one foot in the "instinctive" category and the other in that "learned fear" category.

Here are some of them:

Fear of the Dark

It's interesting to note that very young children aren't afraid of the dark. It's only something that develops as our brains, and by extension our imagination, develops. It is only then that we begin to populate the dark with our fearful imaginings, as we start to conceive of entities that might cause us harm, that might attack us, frighten us, inevitably we populate the shadows and the darkness with those entities. Of course, this runs deep into that fundamental fear — the *Fear of the Unknown*, for where else does the unknown lie, if not in the dark?

Fear of Closed Spaces/Being Trapped/Paralysis

It's worth noting, as above, that very young infants actually find confinement, in the form of "bundling," in which the infant is tightly wrapped up so that she ends up looking like a little mummy, actually quite comforting. Theories suggest that this state imitates the confined environment of the womb.

But as we age and start to feel the need to move around, being restricted and confined becomes not only unpleasant but ultimately deeply disturbing. While there are obviously many people who aren't bothered by tight spaces (note those people who go crawling around in caves) for many of us, the prospect of being confined in tight quarters, unable to move, or having our ability to move restricted, likewise the thought of being physically paralyzed, is a profoundly terrifying one.

Fear of Bees/Stinging Insects
A sub-category of the fear we have of insects, generally. While the grounding, in the form of our fear/discomfort of insects generally, is present regarding bees, wasps, etc., it's inevitably magnified in respect to any stinging or biting insect, and often all it takes is for someone to get stung as a young child for that fear to be fully established, often for a lifetime.

Fears of Thunder and Lightning
A very common childhood fear, and not a surprising one. Extremely loud and sudden explosive noise, bright flashing light, and the whole thing often accompanied by huge winds. This immediately triggers our fight or flight reaction. But, of course, there really isn't much we can do, and it is that helplessness in the face of a relentlessly violent nature that magnifies our fear.

It's not surprising that ancient (and not so ancient) peoples associated thunderstorms with the anger of heaven. There is just something about thunder and lightning that suggests rage and danger, and as young children we respond accordingly. We feel as if we're under attack, and helpless to defend ourselves, and very often carry those reactions with us into adult life.

Fear of Deformity
There's a term known as the "Uncanny Valley" that's used in the realm of CGI or other manufactured images of the Human Figure.

It describes what happens when the image in question comes quite close to being perfectly realistic but not quite close enough. The human observer can tell the difference, and that condition of "close but not quite human" is enough to set off alarm bells in our heads. It's shouting, "Whatever this is, it isn't really human! — It's not one of us!"

Unfortunately, and perhaps tragically, human beings with physical deformities can also trigger that same "uncanny valley" response. This can be something as minor as being "wall-eyed," where you simply don't quite know where the person is looking, or of those born with Down Syndrome, or those with much more dramatic physical injuries or birth defects.

Very young children hardly react at all to the sight of physical deformities and children who are raised by parents who possess even extreme physical deformities don't find them to be unusual or disturbing. It seems clear that part of what makes such things disturbing to us is the need, through experience, to establish certain norms of human appearance and behavior. Once those norms are established through cultural determinants and are more-or-less "locked in," it is only then that those individuals who stray too far from those normative standards will trigger that "uncanny valley" reaction.

LEARNED FEARS

Inevitably, even those fears that we learn have their roots in our deeper shared humanity. Of course, we come into this world with the capacity to feel pain, both physical, mental, and emotional, but inevitably, there's no way to know just what we might face in the world. The dangers and terrors change from place to place and time to time, and so we are well-adapted to change as well. As different things in different times and places hurt and threaten us, so our fears likewise change along with them.

These fears are shaped by who we are, by our personal experiences, by our times, and by the expectations of those around us.

Fear of Heights/Falling

It was thought for a long time that this was an instinctive fear. This was based on research done in 1960 by psychologists E. J. Gibson and R. D. Walk, in which infants were allowed to crawl out across a wide sheet of glass that extended across a sudden drop. Even infants who had never experienced a fall and thus had no "conditioned response" to the danger of falling, nevertheless pulled back from the apparent brink.

But more recent and extensive studies conducted by Karen Adolph, at the Infant Action Lab, now indicate that infants aren't intrinsically afraid, but actually learn to navigate drops and slopes without any particular anxiety or fear response. Thus, individuals who fear heights and falling must learn this reaction through experience later in life.

Fear of Open Spaces

The technical term for this is *agoraphobia*, which also includes the fear of crowds, and of social interactions generally. Just as many people have a fear of closed spaces, being trapped, and of being paralyzed, the Fear of Open Spaces is its mirror image. Agoraphobia also develops in association with *panic attacks*, sudden and often unpredictable attacks of paralyzing terror. It's worth noting that this syndrome is very rarely found in young children. It is one that develops much more frequently later in life. It's often found in the elderly.

What causes it? While it sometimes arises due to *post-traumatic stress syndrome* or in response to stress, there often seems to be no particular reason for it to be found in the sufferer's life history.

It's interesting to note that this condition seems to have a genetic component. Those who suffer from it are likely to have relatives who also suffer from it.

Some of this may relate to the fundamental differences in personality types between introverts and extroverts, those who tend to prefer solitary activities as opposed to those who enjoy social and interactive environments. While there's nothing wrong with being either an introvert or an extrovert, there's a possibility that Agoraphobia may embody an intensification of in-born introverted tendencies.

Apart from that, the underlying causes are obscure.

Fear of Public Speaking/Public Humiliation
It's interesting to note that, for whatever reason, women in general tend to be more fearful than men — with one exception. This is it. Men are more afraid of public speaking, of being compelled to expose themselves (figuratively) before the judgment and potentially, the scorn, of others.

Some of this may reach back to ancient prehistory, to our origins as a tribal species in which our ancestors had to establish relationships of dominance and submission. These hierarchies of dominance and submission often involved ritualized displays as much as actual physical combat; displays in which the defining attributes of confidence, skill, physical strength, health, beauty, intelligence, et al., had to be demonstrated to the members of your pack. By demonstrating this publicly, males achieved dominance or, failing to do so, were humiliated, sometimes to the point of being driven from the pack.

It's possible that, for many men, the prospect of having to present themselves publicly triggers some of those ancient competitive fears — those fears of failure, those fears of public judgement by their peers, the fear of public humiliation and of ostracism. Far better, something whispers from out of the subconscious, to remain silent and anonymous. Let others try and suffer the risks of failure and humiliation, while you stay safe in the shadows . . . .

Fear of Contamination/Contagion

Our feeling of revulsion at the sight, the smell, the touch of various bodily contaminants seems so obvious and inevitable that it's difficult for us to realize that this is, in fact, learned behavior.

Any parent who has raised children from infancy knows very well that babies and toddlers show no revulsion, never mind fear, of excrement, vomit, blood, or decay, not only of the human variety, but of pretty much any other nasty and repulsive material that they might find in their environment.

We respond so dramatically to such things that we fail to realize that there must have been a time in our lives that none of these things bothered us at all. Not the smell of vomit, not the touch of mucous, not the sight of excrement, or the smell of death. We learned, through conditioned response, to be repelled by them, and by extension, to include these things in the broad category of contaminated/contagious things to which we respond with a sense of loathing and horror.

Fear of Being Crushed/Dismembered/Devoured

This particular fear reaches far beyond the general apprehension that we have toward physical harm or death. Nobody wants to be shot or stabbed or to die from a heart attack, but those sorts of bodily assaults are rarely associated with a sense of horror. Having your body torn apart, crushed, or eaten by something, whether by one creature big enough to do it, or by a great many smaller creatures, on the other hand, is genuinely horrifying.

I've grouped all of these different fears together because they have something in common. Obviously, these would all be horribly painful experiences, but there's more to it than that. Fundamental to our sense of self is that we are "Beings," not merely things. A chair is a thing. A piece of meat is a thing. A dismembered arm is a thing. A dead body is a thing.

The sudden and brutal transformation of that "Being," of ourselves, transformed into a mere thing, into crushed flesh, into dismembered limbs, into prey devoured by some other creature — it is that transformation that inspires horror — that brutally triggers that "Sense of Dread."

Fear of Being Lost
An essential part of growing up is moving out of the comfortable and familiar realm of home and family as we start to navigate the larger world beyond. At first, we start to explore that unfamiliar world in the company of others — parents, older siblings, teachers, etc. But eventually, we will set out on our own and face the inevitable disorienting reality of becoming lost. Sometimes, we might be lost in the woods, or on the streets of a town or a city, or else (and sometimes this can be even more frightening) lost in the midst of a crowd, at the beach, or a shopping center, surrounded by countless strangers.

Those early experiences of being suddenly and unexpectedly cut off from friends, family, home, and safety can be terrifyingly disorienting. No string or trail of bread crumbs, no map or compass to guide us back home. We suddenly find ourselves adrift in the world. What can we do?

That fear of being lost and alone follows many of us from early childhood, whether we find ourselves lost in a crowd in bright daylight or lost alone in the woods in the dead of night, the helpless child emerges from the depths of memory — and we are afraid.

It's worth mentioning that the Ancient Greeks had a name for exactly this sort of fear — the sudden and inexplicable terror that came upon travelers in the deep woods at night. They imagined that it was caused by a visitation from their god of the wood, the goat-legged god, Pan, and so it was named after him — *Panic Fear.*

COMMON PHOBIAS

Phobias are intensely paralyzing versions of fears that are broadly experienced. Where do normally experienced fears end and phobias begin? Psychologists generally categorize phobias in terms of their capacity to interfere with daily functioning. If a fear is so intense that it prevents you from living your normal life, then it has risen to the level of a phobia.

But it's important to realize that there is no clear line of demarcation. For any given fear, you will find people at one end of the scale who have absolutely no fear at all (say no fear of snakes) all the way to those who are absolutely paralyzed at anything that even looks like a snake.

Why this broad difference? While some of this may be caused by a traumatic incident or life experience, very few such fears can be traced to this. It's possible (though we really don't know) that fear levels in respect to particular things may simply be a normal human variation, much like height or hair color or temperament. This may account for the fact that, statistically, women tend to be more fearful than men.

So — here are some common phobias. Of course, there are inevitably some fears listed below that we've already talked about:

- Fear of Spiders and Insects
- Fear of Snakes

- Fear of Rats and Mice and other Crawling Things
- Fear of Drowning/Smothering/Choking
- Fear of Being Lost
- Fear of Close Spaces/Paralysis
- Fear of Crowds/People/Open Spaces/Being on Public Display
- Fear of Heights/Falling
- Fear of The Night/The Dark
- Fear of Thunder and Lightning
- Fear of Uncleanliness/Contamination, including:
  Blood
  Vomit
  Excrement
  Mucous
  Pus
  Viscera
  Slime
  Decay/Rotted flesh
  Bodily Infection/Infestation/Parasites

In addition to the above, there are other common phobias, which are, of course, intense versions of more broadly held fears.

Fear of Flying

This is one of the more common phobias, and is also an extremely common fear, above and beyond the common fear of heights and of falling. Why flying in particular? It's speculated that for many people, the lack of control exacerbates this fear — the fact that not only have they been carried to lethal altitudes, but that their fate is in the hands of technology, of weather, of men and women over whom they have no control at all. It is that highly effective combination of "Height + Helplessness" that drives the *Fear of Flying*.

Fear of Dogs/Fierce Animals

More than most fears, this is often triggered by environmental reactions, early experiences with aggressive barking or biting dogs. As young children, our reactions to loud noises are built in, because loud noises in our environment are often associated with danger. It could be anything from a falling tree to a charging rhino to an attacking animal. Thus, a loud, barking dog triggers the Flight-or-Fight reaction, and even if the dog doesn't cause any harm, it impresses itself upon our memory. If it bites, that makes an even greater impression, one that can follow us throughout our lives.

Fear of Blood

It is obvious that many people have little or no fear of blood at all. At the same time, for those who have this fear, it can literally be crippling. It is no exaggeration to say that some people literally pass out at the sight of blood. Yet it is important to realize that this is largely a learned behavior. In frontier societies in which animals are hunted and butchered by every family, it is very rare for people to react with fear at the sight of blood. Quite simply, they have been raised around it and they see it all the time.

Of course, as blood is associated with injury in ourselves and others, it is appropriate that we draw those inevitable associations, but often our alarm at the sight of blood comes more from having seen an exaggerated reaction from those around us as we grew up, from those who rarely saw blood in their daily lives, and as we saw those extreme reactions, we learned those lessons and sometimes learned them too well.

Fear of Shots/Needles/Blades

This is one of the most common phobias around, effecting around fifty million people in the United States alone. Obviously, part of the fear of getting a shot, or of being cut by anything razor-sharp, relates to a very obvious reluctance to having our skin pierced by anything. It injures us. It hurts.

At any rate, it arises early. Young children are terrified at getting shots, and the fear often remains or even intensifies in many adults, becoming a crippling phobia. Some adults will avoid any medical treatment, even life-saving treatment, if it means facing a needle.

Fear of Hospitals/Doctors

Of course, the connection between the fear of getting shots and the fear of hospitals and doctors is obvious, but the broader fear runs deeper. To understand it, it's worth examining and understanding the "rituals" of hospitalization. Patients are made to undress, to wear robes that render them partially naked. They are wheeled around in wheelchairs, even if they are perfectly capable of walking, likewise made to lie in bed, even if there's nothing about their condition that would necessitate their staying in bed.

While there are some vague justifications for doing these things, the main reason is to institute a fundamental change in status, to move someone from being an autonomous person in control of themselves to becoming a "patient," a submissive and largely helpless being who will, ideally, be under the control of the hospital staff. Ultimately, patients are going to have to go through some exceptionally unpleasant, debilitating, painful, and perhaps even crippling experiences while in the hospital. The more they resist, the more they fight back, the harder it will be (from the hospital's perspective) for the staff to do what has to be done.

In response, hospitals institute a series of procedures to render the patient more submissive, more helpless, and more dependent. The hospital staff would say that it is to help them do their jobs more effectively.

But think of it from the perspective of the patient. Remember what makes flying so terrifying for those who fear it? It is the sense of being helpless and out of control. That is exactly the sense that hospitals are trying to create in their patients. Their goal is for patients to surrender their sense of personal autonomy and control to the doctors, nurses, and staff around them. They want you to put yourself in their hands. Their intentions may be benign, but for many people, the less control they have, the more terrifying the experience becomes.

Fortunately, many doctors and some hospitals are changing their views on this approach. But old habits die hard, and many of the rituals of forced submission are still alive and well in the corridors of our hospitals, along with the terror that such places inevitably engender.

Fear of Fire/Being Burned

Humanity's love-hate relationship with fire extends far back into prehistory. In some ways, fire has been essential in the development of civilization. It brought light and warmth into the cold and dark of our ancestors' night. It was instrumental in preparing food, in working metal for tools and weapons, and later in clearing fields for planting. Fire was one of Humanity's earliest faithful servants — but always a dangerous servant, likely to lose control and to turn upon its master.

There has always been a strange dichotomy at the heart of our relationship with fire. Knowing its dangers and its capacity to get out of our control and to spread destruction, as we come to know it, we inevitably fear it. Yet we are also fascinated by it, by its beauty and its power, even by its power to destroy.

There's a reason why people have traditionally stopped to watch a house fire, much as people slow their cars to peek at the scene of a traffic accident. It's more than merely curiosity. We are drawn to the flames, much as we are drawn to a scene of death and destruction, so long as the fire doesn't get too hot, or the danger too close. We are horrified, and yet we are fascinated.

As to the deeper phobias that many people have regarding fire, these can emerge from traumatic exposure to fire early in their lives.

Often though, as with many phobias, they remain unexplained.

NIGHTMARES

We spend around a quarter of our lives asleep, and a quarter of our time asleep is spent in REM (rapid eye movement) or dream sleep.

So why exactly do we sleep? And why do we dream?

There are a number of theories, but what it really comes down to is, though it has been studied and continues to be studied, there is no scientific consensus — nobody really knows. Whatever sleep is, though, we know that it's conserved across broad areas of the animal kingdom.

All mammals and all birds sleep.

Sleep is so well-conserved that aquatic mammals that would drown if they became completely unconscious and certain species of birds that often remain in flight for days or even weeks at a time, have evolved what's known as "uni-hemispherism," that is, one side of the brain sleeps while the other remains wakeful.

All birds and mammals exhibit REM sleep, which means that they also dream.

So why do we dream? Why do other animals and birds dream?

Again, there are a number of theories, but no consensus. For a time, it was theorized that sleep was intended as simply a means of conserving energy, but then we discovered that animals in hibernation also sleep, and in order to do it they actually have to briefly increase their metabolism in order to enter their sleep phase (and this would hardly apply to migrating birds who sleep while in flight), so that explanation obviously won't do.

Though we have no way of knowing what animals may dream about, there is some suggestion that, as with human beings, animals will act out behaviors in their dreams that correspond to similar behaviors that occur during their waking lives. At any rate, experiments studying the brain waves of sleeping and waking animals have found correspondences between the brain waves associated with certain waking activities and the same brain waves experienced by those animals when they're asleep.

We've seen the same thing in dream studies involving human beings.

It may be that what we experience or remember as dreaming is part of the larger process by which temporary memories acquired during the day are sorted and biologically catalogued into permanent memories.

Sleep and dreaming may be the brain's regular and essential sorting and book-keeping period, without which the brain becomes overloaded with uncatalogued material and is finally unable to process anything new.

Though we don't exactly know why, we know that we must sleep and that we must dream. Those who are deprived of them will quite literally die of exhaustion.

That leads to the final question and the one most relevant to us. We all dream, but dreams come in different sorts, and most of us not only have dreams but nightmares.

So what are nightmares? Why do we have them? Unfortunately, the answer is the same.

Many theories, but no consensus. Nobody really knows.

The word itself, "Nightmare," has nothing to do with horses, but comes from the Old English word "mare" meaning a demon or goblin who disturbs our sleep with terrifying dreams.

In various traditions, dreams and nightmares have often had a prophetic character, in which evil dreams are sent to warn us of evil events to come.

More modern approaches have substituted a subconscious or psycho-symbolic significance for dreams and nightmares, in which various dream archetypes are universally representational, such that figures and events in our dreams embody collective stand-ins for Father or Mother, or a variety of human anxieties and desires. While such interpretations are always possible and may give us a useful framework for examining our dreams and nightmares, caution is always advised in respect to all such theories, since falsifying them, if they are actually false (a required hallmark of any valid scientific theory) is exceptionally challenging.

While waking anxieties certainly have an effect on our dreams, it's important to remember that we tend to forget most dreams almost immediately, both good and bad, and that anything that disturbs our sleep will increase the likelihood of our remembering our dreams. So when our days are filled with worries, those worries may not only present themselves in the form of nightmares but also, because they interfere with our sleep, they increase the chances of our remembering those disturbing dreams.

For the purposes of this book, it's worth looking at some of those "nightmare" archetypes. Some of them are familiar, relating as they do, to phobias and to waking fears that we've already discussed.

Yet some of those archetypes seem to be found much more broadly in the realms of our nightmares than we might otherwise expect. Why these particular images and scenarios, as opposed to countless others? Why is it that so many of us share certain categories of nightmares, walk down the same shadow corridors when we sleep?

Again, as with so much about the experience of sleep, there are many theories but nobody really knows for sure.

It may be, as Carl Jung suggests, that many of these dream and nightmare images have deep and universal symbolic significance, his so-called archetypes of the collective unconscious. Again, while these notions may be intriguing and worth further study, it is more than we are capable of exploring here.

The Dream of Reason Produces Monsters — Francisco de Goya

In exploring various Nightmare Motifs, it's important to realize that nightmares encompass not only events, but in a deeper sense, emotions, memories, and even our sense of identity.

That is, we not only dream an experience — say, for instance, a half-open door — but we also "dream" how we feel in response to it, which may be an emotion of stark terror. The door itself may not be intrinsically frightening. Within the dream we may not know, nor ever know what lies behind it.

The fear we feel is part of the dream itself.

In the same way, we may visit some place, in the context of a dream, that we have visited many times before, may meet someone that we know well — and yet all of that too, may simply be part of the dream — memories of events and people that never actually happened outside of the constructed universes of the dreams themselves. We may have the sense of having a dream that we have dreamt many times before, and that too may simply be part of a dream that we have only ever had once and never before.

Even our own identity, within the landscape of dreams, is often changeable, or divided. The sense of simultaneously being within a dream and at the same time observing the events of the dream, including ourselves, is commonplace.

Less commonplace is the experience of genuine duality, of having two unique sets of thoughts, even of two distinct personalities running at the same time, which can also occur during dreams. Our brains consist of two hemispheres, one of which is normally inaccessible to our waking or conscious mind. It's possible that, during dream sleep, there are interactions between these two hemispheres, and briefly, we are able to experience what both of our "selves" — in the sense of both hemispheres of our brains — are thinking and even dreaming, at the same time.

Falling/Heights

Common nightmare motifs frequently incorporate scenarios of falling, vertiginous heights, climbing in dangerous or threatening environments, or combinations of the above.

In the early stages of sleep, dreams of tripping or falling are sometimes associated with a "sleep start." This is a sudden, fearful awakening, accompanied by a sharp twitching of the body known as a "hypnic jerk" or a myoclonic contraction. This abrupt jumping awake, sometimes accompanied by a gasp or other vocalization, appears to be associated with a change in brain wave activity, as the brain moves from one sleep state into a deeper one. That is, as we start to "fall" into a deeper state of sleep, that descent is somehow translated into a literal sense of falling, and the body, especially one that's been primed with caffeine or other stimulants, reacts in this unfortunate way.

There have been some theories that suggest that the pervasive fear of falling in dreams reaches far back to our pre-human tree-dwelling ancestors who had to sleep high up in the limbs of trees and who thus had a keenly instinctive reaction against falling, especially while sleeping. In support of this theory is the observed fact that our hands grip tightly while we sleep, an instinctive reaction that we share with modern tree-dwelling apes, who grab onto tree limbs to hold themselves in place while sleeping.

While this is an intriguing idea, the support for it is nevertheless limited.

What we do know is that the fear of heights and of falling seems to broadly permeate our nightmares across time and culture.

Being Pursued

The place may be familiar or strange. It may be day or night, inside or outside. It may be some place from the familiar present or out of your past, or someplace that you've never seen before, or maybe an amalgam of all of them. The same is true of the Pursuer. It may be someone that you know currently, or someone out of your past, or someone that you've never known, a friend, an enemy, or a stranger. Or the Pursuer may be something inhuman, a predatory animal, an alien, a monster, or a shadowy *something* largely unseen, yet nevertheless terrifying.

You, the Pursued, may be as you normally are, or you may be someone else — perhaps a younger version of yourself, or you as a child — or someone altogether different, or your identity may shift as the dream unfolds.

And as with all dream landscapes, the places and people and beings often change unpredictably as well. What stays the same is that you are being relentlessly pursued, that you are terrified, and that you desperately need to escape.

Inability to Flee, Inability to Run, Heavy Feet

A common adjunct to the nightmare of pursuit is that you, the Pursued, often find that for various reasons within the dreamscape, your ability to escape the Pursuer is impeded in some terrifying way. As you run, you find that your feet suddenly become impossibly heavy, or seem to stick to the ground, as if you were stuck in mud or quicksand. The harder you try to move, the more difficult it becomes. There may be a sense of entanglement, of being generally trapped and unable to move at all, even being unable to breathe.

This sense of being frozen, trapped, or paralyzed is related to the broader experience of "sleep paralysis" which can occur as we slip between waking and sleeping and which we will discuss later.

What is worth mentioning though, is how familiar this particular scenario is to those who regularly watch horror movies. That is, the Pursuer, whether human or inhuman, comes on slowly, loping, limping, and the desperate Pursued, often runs as fast as they can, and yet somehow — however slowly the Pursuer advances and however fast the Pursued runs (despite the occasional and inevitable trip) — the oncoming Menace inevitably closes the distance. This is the Logic of a Nightmare, and it comes straight from our own nightmares of pursuit and our inability to escape.

Being Late/Being Lost/Not Knowing Where to Go (Late for Class)
This is one of our most common nightmares and is interesting because it combines both fundamental and instinctive fears, that of disorientation and the fear of being lost with the learned fears that relate to social concerns; meeting obligations such as showing up on time, knowing where your proper classes are, having prepared for that test that you were supposed to take, being where you're supposed to be when you're supposed to be there, all of those deep fears and anxieties that relate to our place in our particular social order. That's especially true as we grow up into that social order and have to face all of the pressures that are put upon us to conform to the demands of achievement: test-taking, schedules, going to new strange places, etc.

For the majority of us, we feel safe at home in the world of familiar things, and by extension, the world outside is new, strange, and potentially dangerous. It is both tempting and threatening. The path to mastering that world carries with it a set of stereotypical anxieties and fears that often express themselves in the form of nightmares.

The "late for class" nightmare, the "Final Exam that you haven't studied for" nightmare, the "Can't find my classroom" nightmare, all of these and countless variations are expressions of those enduring anxieties.

Bodily Distortion/Decay or Identity Change
One of the more common aspects of dreams, as I've indicated above, is the fundamentally changeable nature of people, places, and things within the dream landscape. Most of these transformations are non-threatening or even joyful. One can have dreams in which one is younger, or a child again (presuming that one had a pleasant childhood), or an animal, or some admired person, or possessed of godlike powers. Those who have died might be alive in our dreams. We may revisit places and people who have long departed.

It's common to speak of our "dreams coming true" and there are whole categories of "wish fulfilment" dreams to which that expression applies.

But on the other hand, there are also dreams that we never want to come true; transformations of our bodies, our identities, and the identities of those we know and love in ways that can be profoundly disturbing. These include changes in physical scale; we may find ourselves giants or dwarves, or some parts of our bodies — hands, arms, legs, eyes, fingers — distorted in size. In some nightmares, this distortion tends to focus on one side of the body, with eyes and head swollen or limbs or fingers swollen out of proportion on only one side.

Not only may we find that our bodies have changed physically

— aging, decaying, or no longer working as they should — but we may also find ourselves possessed of forbidden desires and feelings that are not our own, or at any rate, desires that our conscious minds do not recognize or acknowledge. We may experience rage, lust, fear, or hatred and act upon those emotions, directing them toward Others, sometimes familiar Others, or Others who have been transformed, or Strangers who may be surrogates for those we know, or simply Unknown Others who populate the mysterious landscapes of our nightmares.

More disturbing still is the inevitable fact that, as in all nightmares, there is a sense of reality to the impossibilities of the dream world. We may react with horror at who we are, how we look, what we feel, how we act — but yet, doesn't it all seem as if it has always been this way, will always be this way?

Losing or Breaking Teeth
A common adjunct to the above category of bodily distortion are nightmares involving the losing or breaking of teeth, often our own teeth, sometimes those of others. Nightmares may involve teeth becoming loose, falling out, being displaced in our mouths, coming loose in the midst of embarrassing social situations, or our discovering that our teeth are missing or oddly changed or distorted, too small or too large.

Why all of these dreams about teeth? Well, one obvious possibility reaches back to our Sensory Homunculus: our teeth are among the most highly innervated parts of our bodies, and because they are so highly sensitive and thus lay claim to a larger portion of our brain's sensory landscape in our waking life, perhaps they also demand a higher degree of our brain's attention in the realms of our dreams.

There may be an association between these "tooth" dreams and night-time bruxism, or tooth grinding, which may affect as much as 50% of the population (growing less as we grow older), but what connection there may be, if any, is purely speculation.

Blood/Bodily Fluids
Our waking fear and revulsion of blood and other bodily fluids and materials — mucous, vomit, excreta, et al. — often presents itself in the transgressive territory of our nightmares. Scenarios involving finding ourselves bleeding, or others bleeding, touching or being touched or covered by blood or other unwholesome bodily materials, or even consuming these things, or often more terrible still, realizing after the fact that one has eaten or is eating something unwholesome, are all common nightmare motifs.

Sexual Transformation/Violation/Forbidden Acts
Here, of course, the ultimate transgressive realm and the territory that is often rarely touched upon consciously, or if so, is often cloaked in feelings of shame and guilt, often rears its head in our nightmares.

This includes the whole range of forbidden sexual relations, ranging from adultery, to homosexual acts (presuming that one considers such acts to be forbidden), to relations with children or animals. Sometimes we may be in the midst of such acts ourselves or may be witnessing someone else engaging in them. We may be the victim or the victimizer, finding ourselves experiencing the terror and shame of violation, or — and perhaps this is even more disturbing — experiencing the terrible desires of the aggressor. Or, as sometimes happens in dreams, we may experience both at the same time, or we may observe from some perspective removed from the action as our "Dream Self" engages in some activity that the "Watching Self" finds horrifying, but has no power to stop.

Night Terrors

Night Terrors or Sleep Terrors are a dramatic and frightening phenomenon different from conventional nightmares. Most notably, they don't occur during traditional REM (rapid eye movement) sleep, which is the time when we dream. Nightmares, of course, are simply a kind of dream. So, it is clear that we experience vivid dream-like and nightmare experiences outside of the times that are associated with traditional dreaming.

Night Terrors, as a rule, tend to happen either early in sleep or near awakening, and are often associated with sleep walking. In fact, they seem to be a sub-category of sleep-walking.

The sufferers (and the majority are children) often begin an episode by screaming, thrashing in bed, sitting up with eyes wide open in terror, sometimes getting out of bed and moving around the house. But they are not awake, and strongly resist being restrained or awakened.

What the internal experience of Night Terrors may be is obscure as the sufferers don't seem to remember the experience. Fortunately, Night Terrors don't seem to have any lasting negative effects, despite how shocking they may be to those who have to live through them.

Sleep Walking

Night Terrors are, obviously, associated with the larger phenomenon of Sleep Walking, but what causes that?

To understand it, we need to look at how the brain behaves when we sleep. During sleep, we have experiences that correspond to waking activities. When we do, the parts of the brain that correlate to those actions are activated. We "dream" of walking, so the brain sends signals to our legs, telling them to walk.

So why don't we? That's because, as we pass into sleep, the brain activates a system that, in essence, paralyzes the body, preventing it from carrying out the brain's instructions.

But sometimes that system goes wrong. And when it does, the instructions manage to go through, and though we continue to sleep, our bodies get up and act out, not only walking but sometimes speaking, writing, having sexual relations — a whole range of behaviors.

It is interesting to note that Sleep Walking, like Night Terrors, doesn't occur during REM sleep, so even though we are carrying out, in some fashion, experiences in our sleep state, these are not "dreams" in the traditional sense, in the same way that Night Terrors are not nightmares in the traditional sense.

Sleep Paralysis/Feelings of Suffocation
In the same way that the mechanism which paralyzes the sleeping body can go wrong, thus permitting Sleep Walking, it also sometimes goes wrong in the opposite way. That is, the Sleeper begins to wake, but the body remains paralyzed.

The result, which can last from seconds to minutes can lead to a terrifying sense of suffocation, a feeling of pressure on the chest. It's sometimes accompanied by a feeling of a terrifying "presence," as if somebody or something is literally pressing down on top of you. Thus we get the myth of the "night hag," a hideous supernatural visitant that crouches down on top of the sleeper's chest during the night. Many stories will draw upon a variety of the above elements.

List: Some of your favorite horror movies that rely on instinctive, learned, and nightmare fears.

List: One or more nightmares of yours that might form the basis of a scary scene.

Write: a brief scene that employs some of the above fears.

3

FEAR ITSELF, PART THREE

FEARS BASED
IN CULTURE

Horror is the natural reaction to the last 5,000 years of History.

Robert Anton Wilson

Only human beings have "culture" as the term is generally understood. It refers to the expression of the broadly held beliefs, myths, art, taboos, and social practices of a given people. Inevitably, many of our collective hopes, our aspirations, and also our fears emerge from the culture of which we are a part.

For instance, it's not surprising that people who are part of a culture that is strongly oriented toward Fundamentalist Christianity and a belief in a literal Satan often fear the tortures of Hell.

Conversely, in traditional cultures that possess a strong belief in curses tend to have a comparable fear of witches and witchcraft.

These are, of course, learned fears, but they belong in a category of their own. We are social animals and these are "social fears," in the sense that they emerge from our place in a larger society.

PARANOID FEARS

When we talk about Paranoid fears, it's important to make clear that we are not talking about paranoid schizophrenia, which is a specific form of mental illness.

However, the paranoid form of schizophrenia is characterized by certain kinds of delusions and obsessions which are often reflected in fears and anxieties that are broadly shared by the surrounding society of which the sufferers are a part. It is those latter fears that we are going to explore in this section.

Fear of Conspiracies

Conspiracies lie at the heart of Paranoid Fear, and as modern society becomes ever more interconnected, the power of technology to spread these conspiratorial memes has grown exponentially.

What seems to be at the root of such fears? In some sense, the tendency to see conspiracies is a response to an even deeper fear, the fear that we may be in a fundamentally disordered and meaningless universe. It is terrifying to imagine that death and injustice arise through random forces and random acts. On the other hand, there is some comfort in the notion that such actions are the result of broad, unknown, malicious, perhaps even alien or supernatural forces, that are working secretly to bring them about. If that is the case, in principle, those forces can be unmasked, exposed, and fought.

Conspiracies knit together often unrelated events, such as school shootings, or incidents of child sex abuse, into a single, broadly connected network of malignant operators. Instead of simply being an accumulation of tragedies, they become a puzzle capable of being solved.

The problem is that the threads of connection are often purely imaginary. Human beings are pattern-seeking animals and unfortunately, like seeing animals in drifting clouds or the face of Jesus on a piece of toast, the pattern-seeking mechanism can also cause us to see connections between events that simply aren't there.

Those who retreat to a world of conspiracies inevitably find themselves living in a realm in which countless organizations, governments, businesses, religions, are spinning webs of lies around them all the time.

To be a conspiracy theorist is very much like living in John Carpenter's movie *They Live* (1988), in which the world has been invaded by aliens indistinguishable from normal human beings, unless you happen to have a pair of special glasses that reveal their true nightmare form — only in our world, the real world, nobody has the glasses.

You just have to rely on a variety of arbitrarily chosen Authority Figures to tell you who to trust and who the "aliens" are.

The result is that, in backing away from that fear of a disordered world, the Conspiracy Theorist ends up backing into a world that is, in many ways, far more terrifying — a world in which no institution, no government, no media, no family member, no person, can ever be completely trusted.

In fact, for the Ultimate Conspiracy Theorist, we may not even be able to trust ourselves.

Fear of Possession/Mind Control

The concept of possession, either by human, demonic, or animal spirits, is an ancient one, reaching back in various forms as far as ancient Egypt and Greece, and was (and still is) broadly believed across the world. Not all such concepts of possession are necessarily malignant. Some traditions involve connecting to animal or human spirits in order to gain strength or wisdom. But in many traditions, such possession is most definitely involuntary and destructive.

The human body is invaded by some external force, the purpose of which is to control, dominate, and ultimately to destroy the body and to steal or corrupt the soul of the victim.

In the West, we are familiar with the concept of Demonic Possession and Exorcism, concepts that reach back to accounts in the Christian Bible.

Islam also has a tradition of victims being possessed by Jinns, spirits that rank lower than angels but have the power to appear as human beings or animals. But it's important to note that Jinns, unlike demons, are not inherently evil and so their motivations for possessing human beings can vary from case to case.

Traditional eastern religions may also contain notions of spirit possession in less familiar forms.

In addition to the notion of possession as we traditionally understand it, is the notion of *mind control*, the sense that either we, or those we know, have fallen under the control of someone else or of some malign influence.

This notion may have its root either in the Supernatural — again, the notion that either our minds or the minds of others are being controlled by demonic or Unnatural agencies — or in the Pseudo-natural realm. I say "pseudo-natural" because, insofar as we know, the ability of natural or human forces to actually control the human mind (say, through hypnotic suggestion or "brain-washing") is extremely limited.

So the fear of mind control is expressed in the common ideas that some Government (either our own or a Foreign Power) has acquired some means by which they have taken control, either of a select few, or of the population generally. Or perhaps these are Malevolent Aliens who are controlling us for purposes of their own. They may have already taken over the world and are in control of the World's Governments, or perhaps the invasion is underway, or has just begun.

Remember the *Fear of Flying* and what lies at its root? The Sense of Helplessness. In many respects we find the same thing lurking at the heart of the fears related to Mind Control. As people feel less in control of their communities, of their country, of their destiny, even of themselves, as they start to feel like strangers in a strange land, it isn't surprising that they start to feel as if there are forces — intelligent and malevolent forces — at work bringing this all about. Evil Forces controlling the Government. Evil Forces Controlling the Church. Evil Forces controlling the Military. Evil Forces behind Child Sex Abuse and School Shootings. Evil Forces controlling "Us." Both of these ideas, Possession and Mind Control, are connected. They are linked by the deep fear that someone we know, perhaps someone we are close to or care about deeply, has suddenly become a malevolent stranger. Or even more terrifying, the fear that we have become a stranger to ourselves; that we no longer control our own actions, that our thoughts, feelings, even our memories, are no longer our own.

Fear of Secret Sinister Meanings, Codes, Languages, Connections
We spoke earlier in the section dealing with Conspiracies, about the tendency of the human mind to seek out connections in the world. This can, of course, help us to survive. The ability to see and understand connections in the world is part of why humans are as successful as we are. But, inevitably, there's a downside. Because we are as fine-tuned as we are to recognize connections in the world, we will often see them when they are actually not really there.

This mental "fine-tuning" works in a number of different ways. For instance, our brains are built to recognize human faces. So, we will inevitably see them in all sorts of places where they aren't: in clouds, in wood grain, in shadows, or in the patterns of color our eyes make in the dark.

In the same way, we are conditioned to react to the sound of our name. That's why we can pick out someone calling for us in the midst of a crowded room. But in the same way, it's easy to "hear" our name being spoken in that same crowded room, even when it hasn't been. Is someone talking about us? What are they saying? Why are they laughing?

Depending on what your name happens to be, your brain can interpret even purely natural sounds as someone calling your name. "Neal" happens to be one of those names, and on more than one occasion, the author, completely alone in his office, has heard his name being spoken, whispered, called — when there was simply no one there. An auditory hallucination? No. Our daily life is full of little random sounds, coming from outside, coming from around the house (or if you have a couple of dogs, coming from them).

It's just that, every so often, one of those countless sounds happens to come just close enough to the sound of a human name to trigger that reaction, just as that shape in the cloud or in the shadows comes close enough to trigger the reaction that says "that's a face."

This pattern-seeking also leads us astray as we tend to see letters, numbers, and even words in nature: imprinted in layers of rocks, worked into the bark of trees, in cloud formations, in the wings of butterflies, essentially wherever we look. There's a great temptation to see intention in such things. Is the conclusion that these letters hidden in the natural world are the sign of some Higher Power undermined by the fact that nature not only provides us with the letters of the Roman alphabet, but also with the Hebrew, Arabic, and Chinese alphabets as well? What exactly are all of those random letters attempting to convey?

Or is it simply that our letters are geometrically simple and easily reproducible forms, most of which were originally derived from the shapes of Nature itself? Is it really surprising then, that

Nature, with its almost limitless diversity of forms will, by chance alone, occasionally produce those alphabetic shapes, in much the same way that it is able to produce approximations of the human face and the form or the shapes of animals or familiar objects?

Given the above, our pattern-seeking way of thinking has led people to the notion that hidden meanings or secret codes have been worked into either our everyday world or into our sacred texts. If only one could decode these hidden meanings, one could either understand the real, hidden meaning of the world, or perhaps even foretell the future.

Numerology is one such practice, and an ancient one. It is based on the notion that every letter has a corresponding number and that various practices allow one, through the study and manipulation of those numbers, to gain a mystical understanding of people, events, and the future.

The Bible Code, presented in a book by Michael Drosnin in 1997, is another approach to attempting to manipulate letters, in this case the letters of the original Hebrew Bible, as a means to foretell the future. It suggests that by setting the Hebrew letters of the Bible in a graph and reading them at particular intervals, say every tenth letter, every twentieth letter, every fiftieth letter or what-have-you — perhaps left to right, or right to left, or diagonally — one might come up with some arrangements that contain meaningful information about the future.

There are a few problems with this. First of all, interpretation is difficult because the original Hebrew has no vowels, so one has a great deal of flexibility in assigning contemporary meaning to ancient vowel-free wording. Second, it's easy to score a hit when what's been predicted has already happened. It's much harder, using this method, to uncover predictions for things that have not yet happened.

Finally, one can actually use this method with pretty much any book and also derive similar "prophetic" statements. But it's unlikely that Herman Melville intended to predict the future when he was writing *Moby Dick*.

Most likely, this is another example of pattern-seeking behavior gone awry — of finding patterns where none actually exist.

Of course, some may find comfort in the notion of fulfilled prophecy, of the confirmation of ancient, sacred texts, and there's no intention here to address that. Rather, the goal is to look at the other side of that coin.

Namely, there can be a profound sense of fear at that prospect of secret messages hidden in the sacred texts with which we are familiar, and the possibility that those hidden messages may carry dire or even apocalyptic news.

Likewise, the notion that those around us may be communicating in ways that we don't fully understand, using "code" of one kind or another, or that the books or newspapers or the digital media that we use on a daily basis may also be carrying some secret, coded messages or information of which we are unaware.

Thus, we have all of the fears associated with the "Dark Web."

Of course, the "Dark Web" itself is real. It refers to the whole range of unindexed web sites, and within that realm are all of the illegal and illicit sites that involve the sale of drugs, guns, hacked websites, stolen credit cards, illegal pornography — essentially everything nasty and forbidden that the human mind can imagine and that someone else has figured out how to monetize and put up on a web site.

But however nasty something may be in reality, inevitably our fears have the ability to make it nastier still. So, we populate the Dark Web with the world-wide Satanic Network, with Snuff Films, and World-Wide Government Conspiracies.

Our fears inevitably grow in the dark. The Internet and the Dark Web may very well be the biggest and most expressive form of modern Darkness, and it is there that our Contemporary Fears seem to grow and spread more quickly than anywhere else.

OTHER CULTURE-BASED FEARS

Fear of Intruders/Home Invasion

The terror at the prospect of threatening strangers invading our private spaces — not only our homes, but the still-more private spaces within our homes, our bedrooms and bathrooms — lies at the heart of the *Sense of Dread*. Our homes are the places we feel safe and protected. Within the home, we specifically reserve our bedrooms and bathrooms for our most vulnerable and private activities. It is the sudden and unexpected penetration of those safe spaces that creates that sense of horror — that Sense of Dread.

There are countless examples in movies and in fiction in which the home, the bedroom, and the bathroom, have been chosen as the location for a scene of terror. Think of the shower scene in Alfred Hitchcock's *Psycho* (1960), the "horse head" scene in Francis Ford Coppola's *The Godfather* (1974), the besieged houses in George Romero's *Night of the Living Dead* (1968) and Alfred Hitchcock's *The Birds* (1963), among countless others.

There are always places where we expect to be safe, and other places where we expect to face danger — but when danger unexpectedly confronts us in the places where we expect to be safe — the emotion that results is horror.

So effective is the fear engendered by the notion of home invasion that it has become its own sub-genre, producing movies such as William Wyler's *The Desperate Hours* (1955), Michael Haneke's *Funny Games* (1997), remade by the same director in 2007, David

Fincher's *Panic Room* (2002), and Bryan Bertino's *The Strangers* (2008).

Fear of Clowns

There's a famous quote attributed to the great silent actor, Lon Chaney, "There's nothing funny about a clown at midnight."

Inevitably, we would be disturbed at the prospect of a Figure of Fun showing up in a time or a place where it didn't belong. This is central to the notion of the Sense of Dread.

But the fear engendered by clowns runs even deeper than that. We look to the human face as the key conveyor of human emotion. The fact that the Clown's face is painted on — the painted smile, the painted frown, concealing the real emotions beneath — makes for a potentially disturbing dichotomy. Being confronted by a painted face is much the same as being confronted by someone wearing a mask that hides the real face and thus, the real feelings and real appearance beneath.

The Clown, intended to be a figure of fun, can appear to be the Perpetual Stranger, carrying the inherently threatening character possessed by all Strangers.

In addition, the painted face gives the human face beneath an appearance of something that is decidedly less than fully human, thus pushing Clowns into that "uncanny valley" realm that's been previously discussed.

All in all, clowns have always had one foot firmly planted in the realm of our nightmares.

Fear of Madness (in Ourselves and Others)

Among our most fundamental inviolate spaces is the "Self." That's why the fear of possession or mind control is so persuasive. But there is a deeper, and in many ways a more grounded fear, relating to the undermining of our Sense of Self, and that is the fear of madness, of our loss of Self or the loss of those we care about to the ravages of mental illness.

Those familiar to us may become strangers. Friends may become enemies. Those that love us may suddenly hate or fear us. Or perhaps (and this may be even more terrifying) the World Itself may become an unknown and terrifying place if we become the victims of mental illness. The laws of nature, cause and effect, the whole world, may suddenly be revealed, in some unpredictable way, to be fundamentally different from how we have always imagined it to be. And if our own ability to perceive the world, to analyze it, to trust our perceptions, our memories, our capacity to reason, cannot be trusted, by what yard stick can we ever even judge whether we are insane living in a sane world — or just maybe we are sane and the world itself has gone mad?

Fear of Size Distortion
World mythology is replete with tales not only of giants but of "little people," both of whom have always haunted the dark corners of our tales, ancient and modern, and of our fears.

Most of us are familiar with the giants out of mythology: Atlas, who held up the world, the Titans, and the Cyclops Polyphemus out of Greek mythology, the Anakim and Goliath from the Hebrew Bible, Cormoran and Gogmagog from Celtic mythology, and the Frost Giants of Norse mythology. Most other ancient cultures also have tales of giants, both good and bad.

It's interesting to note that the story of the man-eating Polyphemus recounted in *The Odyssey* is not the only mythical account of men being devoured by giants — or even by the human-like gods of the ancients.

The fear of Giant Human or Semi-Human Beings often seems

to go hand-in-hand with the fear of being eaten alive. While one might ascribe such a fear as understandable to peoples who lived side by side with large predatory animals, it's worth noting that occupants of civilized societies, who are unlikely to see such predators outside of a zoo, nevertheless share the horror of being eaten alive, of being treated as a cat treats a mouse, and we still find such narratives as terrifying as our ancestors did.

The "Little People" — the opposite side of the "giant" coin is equally familiar as cultures all around the world have myths and stories of tiny, often distorted Human Beings, sometimes malevolent, such as Goblins, Selkies, or Trows, who steal away our children or substitute changelings, or merely mischievous creatures who disarrange our houses at night or trick travelers on lonely roads or hills, such as Leprechauns, Elves, Pixies, and Sprites. At worst, the Little People can be terrifying, at best they are rarely fully benign. Contact with such magical beings often carries a risk, the chance of being lured into some desperate venture, of trading away something essentially human, losing a piece of one's soul.

Most interesting of all is the modern equivalent of the "Little People." I'm speaking, of course, of the "Grey," the contemporary vision of the visitor from Outer Space. It's worth noting that early descriptions of the occupants of UFOs were of various kinds — Lizard People, Tall, Blonde People, Goblin-like Creatures, Moth-Winged Aliens, and other variants — before settling on the classic slim, small boned, long necked, large-headed, large-eyed, small-mouthed beings that we now associate with UFO visitations.

As with other mythic accounts of "Little People," these beings are sometimes benign, sometimes mischievous, and sometimes terrifying. Just as the Trolls and Goblins of ancient stories were responsible for kidnapping travelers and children, so the "Greys" of our modern pseudo-scientific mythology do the same thing.

Some accounts have even endowed them with literally magical qualities, for instance, the ability to walk through walls.

It is interesting to note that ancient fears are often reconfigured into a contemporary form. The fear of being possessed by Satan is reconfigured into a fear of being mind-controlled by the C.I.A. Fear of being stolen away by Goblins or the "Little People" has been transfigured into a fear of being kidnapped and experimented on by space aliens.

Fear of Rape/Sex-Based Menacing/Coercion
Sexual relations are among the most intimate of all human associations. Thus, necessarily, we are at our most exposed and vulnerable, both physically and emotionally, when we relate to others sexually. We are exposed in the sense of being partially or completely naked. Parts of our bodies that are normally "untouchable" are exposed. We invite highly intimate physical contact or penetration. The experience itself often involves the most intense physical, sometimes even painful sensations.

And in virtually all societies, sexual contact is cloaked in moral, religious, and societal taboos. We are allowed and sometimes encouraged to do things during sex that we are forbidden to do under virtually any other conditions. It all seems so thoroughly "wrong" — in fact, many of us grow up being told that it is wrong — and then we find ourselves in a situation where, whether within the acceptable bounds of our particular culture or otherwise, we all pretty much find ourselves doing it.

Of all of the virtually universal activities in which human beings engage, sexuality is more permeated with the sense of The Forbidden than any other — the other, of course, being Violence.

Our Fears, our Desires, and also our Insecurities related in various ways to Sexuality and the Sex act, inevitably permeate both the literature and the Cinema of Horror. Chief among these, inevitably, is Sexual Violence, the act of Rape, or of Sex that is coerced, whether through threat, through Mind Control, or Possession.

Fear of Mutilation/Torture/Cannibalism/Death

Of course, our fear of pain is very much born with us, as are all of the related prospects of injury and physical harm, not only to ourselves but to those around us. It's important to understand though, that things like the sight of death, suffering, and injury, whether to animals or to other people is largely a matter of socialization.

Whether it is the killing of animals through hunting, through animal sacrifice, or human killing in warfare, or through human sacrifice — all of these things have been common down through history. Ritual Cannibalism has also played a part in various cultural and religious rites. Even practices that strike us as the most extreme form of human abomination — the torture and killing of children — was routinely practiced as part of various religious rituals.

In the same way, self-mutilation or the ritual mutilation of others has also been practiced historically, without any particular fear or horror being attached to it at all.

One need only remember the atrocities of the Roman Arena, perpetrated largely as a kind of grotesque form of public entertainment, including helpless victims being fed alive to animals, burned alive, crucified, women raped to death by bulls — all while the gathered crowds cheered. Nothing to be afraid of here — unless you happen to be one of the "performers."

Here lies the terrifying dichotomy of our fear relating to mutilation, to torture, and even to death. That is why we find this category here, among the fears based in culture, rather than where you might expect it, among the instinctive fears. It is because, overwhelmingly, how we as individuals react to violence — to killing, to physical harm caused to others, and even to the prospect of harm and death directed against ourselves — is intimately connected to the way that these concepts are viewed within the larger community of which we are a part.

If child sacrifice is normal in our world, then for the most part, we consider it to be normal and acceptable.

If a widow being burned alive on the same pyre with her dead husband is normal in our world, then, for the most part, we likewise consider it to be normal and acceptable.

If spectacles of murder and torture are considered to be an enjoyable form of popular entertainment in our world, chances are we'll join in and find it to be enjoyable ourselves.

As with various sexual practices, we can see that what horrifies, repels, and disgusts the members of one culture at a given time seems quite normal and reasonable to members of a different culture at a different time.

How do we then account for the effect of our instinctive fears? Fear of blood? Our instinctive reaction to pain? Don't we, after all, have an instinct for self-preservation? Don't we fear death instinctively?

The reality is much more complicated, because we are much more complicated organisms in which our in-born drives are often at odds with, and thus amenable to being shaped and influenced by, the environments of personal experience and culture.

We have nurturing instincts and aggressive instincts, the instinct to dominate and the instinct to submit. Various conflicting drives and desires are available to be shaped by the forces of the Family, the Tribe, and the Social Groups of which we are a part — which may, themselves be at odds.

Our Family may pull us in one direction, our Faith in another, the Nation in yet another, while our own personal and unique

Fears and Longings may drive us in an altogether different direction. In the end, we are more than simply the sum of what we have inherited from Nature and how our environment seeks to shape us. There is a sort of alchemy that occurs within the developing human mind that yields results that may be altogether unexpected — that may produce geniuses of intellect, art, spirit, or even of evil.

If we were universally repelled by the notion of torture, or cannibalism, or murder, then they would not loom as large as they do within the dark realms of our worst fears. We don't simply fear them because we fear being their object. Obviously, most of us don't want to be tortured, nor killed, nor eaten. I say "most of us" because obviously, there are masochists, both conscious or otherwise, who do arrange things so that they will suffer (the reasons are often complicated), as well as those who, again for various reasons, want to be killed. There have even been cases of people who not only wanted to be killed but who specifically wanted to be killed and cannibalized and have actively sought out people willing to help them accomplish this (hard to tell how one would have "enjoyed" the benefits of such an agreement, never mind enforced it).

But we also fear these things because they loom within many of us as dark temptations. The urge to commit acts of violence, to harm others, to make people suffer, to kill — even, though obviously much less common, to commit acts of cannibalism. All of these things, on some level, are part of our collective human experience.

The tendency is to refer to the people who commit these horrible acts as "monsters" — to describe the acts themselves as "monstrous." But the truth is that they are all too terribly human; the cruelties of parents to their children, the atrocities of war, the systematic use of torture by the State and the Church, the brutalities of genocide, the crimes of the serial killer, the pedophile, and the sexual sadist. None of these are "inhuman" acts. They are all too human.

They belong to us, though we'd like to disown them. And that is one of the reasons we fear them.

Fear of Victimization of the Helpless
Between our instincts, which encourage most of us toward nurturing our young, and toward caring and supporting our close kin, and the vast majority of cultures which support those underlying instincts, one sees that most stable societies have incentivized our built-in desire to care for the young, the old and the helpless amongst us.

In the preface to the law code of Ur-Nammu, created around the year 2050 B.C., the oldest surviving code of law in existence, the King, Ur-Nammu is credited, during his reign (among other things) for this: "The orphan was not delivered up to the rich man; the widow was not delivered up to the mighty man; the man of one shekel was not delivered up to the man of one mina."

In describing this powerful King in the ancient pagan world, he was lauded for protecting the helpless child, the poor, and the widowed.

This thread runs deep. The prospect of harm directed at those that we consider to be the helpless among us stirs not only our sense of outrage, but also our deepest fears. It is not only that we value our own children and our own parents, it is that we ourselves were once children. We were once the helpless ones. And seeing our own relatives grow older, becoming helpless, we cannot help but see, in them, our own future.

In the same way, even the wealthiest and most powerful among us are subject to the winds of fate and fortune. The rich may become poor. The healthy may become sick or crippled. And, if they live long enough, the young will become old.

Inevitably, narratives of threat or harm directed against the traditionally weak or helpless — against Children, the Elderly, the Handicapped, the Blind, and traditionally against Women, who have been viewed as less able to defend themselves than Men — have always produced, and still produce, a powerful reaction. Such narratives, images, scenes, and sequences generally have a much greater effect on a reader or viewer than a comparable scene in which the victim is an otherwise healthy adult male.

Inevitably, of course, modern movies seek to undermine the stereotypes of Women, the Handicapped, the Elderly or even Children as being "helpless" — but even so, when they are shown in danger, it still presses the same button.

Fear of the Helpless as "Victimizers"
As is often the case, we experience the Sense of Dread when our normal expectations are suddenly subverted. Thus, when those that are usually depicted as helpless, those that we love and seek to protect suddenly become a source of danger or menace, the result can be profoundly terrifying.

Horror Cinema has more than its share of terrifying children ranging from Rhoda, the blonde-haired, braided, and murderous daughter of Mervyn LeRoy's *The Bad Seed* (1956), to the possessed Regan MacNeil of William Friedkin's *The Exorcist* (1973), to Damien of Richard Donner's *The Omen* (1976), to the terrifying, glowing-eyed, mind-controlling children of Wolf Rilla's *Village of the Damned* (1960) and Anton Leader's *Children of the Damned* (1964).

Then there's a whole genre of "killer kid" movies, including Sean MacGregor and David Sheldon's *The Devil Times Five* (1974), Narcisco Serrador's *Who Can Kill a Child?* (1976), and Fritz Kiersch's *Children of the Corn* (1984) based on the Stephen King short story, along with its various sequels.

There are, of course, many others — including, more recently, the terrifying Blind Man in Fede Álvarez' *Don't Breathe* (2016).

Fear of Religious-Based Taboos
Every Culture is hemmed in on all sides by a variety of taboos — restrictions of various sorts, some of which loom large in our lives, some of which are almost invisible, either by virtue of seeming self-evident or due to their universal acceptance within a given society.

It is all the more shocking when someone breaks those rules that are never questioned — when they break rules that we don't even realize are rules at all.

Of course, not every taboo necessarily inspires the Sense of Dread. Virtually every culture, for instance, has taboos regarding appropriate dress and nudity and sexuality, but violations of those taboos (with a few exceptions) rarely create any sense of fear or dread.

Taboos relating to religious matters, on the other hand, inevitably touch on issues that affect life and death, our place in the universe, and the fate of our spiritual existence. Thus, the violation of religious taboos very frequently touches the Nerve of Fear. We fear God's wrath. We fear Hell. We fear the judgment of our fellow believers.

Religious Taboos include, of course, all of the vast minutiae of religious law, both codified and folk law, both monotheistic and pagan, curses, witchcraft, demonic possession, the violation of holy places and objects, Secret Knowledge or Forbidden Rituals, Satanism, as well as the entire lore regarding the End of Days.

As with many things that touch upon that Sense of Dread, what much of the above list has in common is, once again, the notion of the Forbidden.

Religions define our place in the cosmos, locate us in the context of a broader moral universe — where we have come from, where we should be, where we are bound, what we ought to do, how we should live — and also, those things that we shouldn't do, shouldn't say, shouldn't think or feel, places we shouldn't go, words that shouldn't be spoken, lines that shouldn't be crossed.

Cross those lines, speak those words, think those thoughts, perform those rituals, invoke those Forbidden Forces, and you have entered into the Realms of Darkness or, perhaps even worse, brought Darkness into our own world.

Fear of Religious Figures or Institutions Being Attacked or Corrupted

Along different lines, we have traditionally looked to our Religious Institutions and Religious Figures as emblematic of dependability, reliability, and trustworthiness (though perhaps a bit less in recent years than in the past). In a world that is constantly changing, we often look to those institutions and those that represent them, as hallmarks of stability, something that we can depend on in times of trouble, loss or grief.

So what happens when those Institutions and the Men and Women within them are shown to be vulnerable to outside forces, corrupt, perhaps even evil — not at all what we thought? Maybe there are Malevolent Influences at work within them. Perhaps Forces of Evil that have, unbeknownst to us, invaded, penetrated, or corrupted the very institutions that we look to for moral guidance? The sheep are revealed to be wolves in disguise — or maybe something worse.

For True Believers, their religious commitments are fundamental. When they come into question, the entire nature of their lives, of the world itself, begins to come apart. If those commitments cannot be trusted, then nothing can. For the deeply religious, it is the inability to fully confront that possibility (a phenomenon known as cognitive dissonance) that awakens a profound Sense of Dread.

Fear of Authority Figures or Institutions Being Attacked or Corrupted

In the same way that many of us have traditionally invested our trust and belief in Religious Institutions and Authority Figures, the same is true for our Government Institutions and Authority Figures. Even within our own current, highly polarized state of affairs, for many of us Party Loyalties or political philosophies and individuals who we view as representational of those Parties or philosophies have stepped up to serve the purpose that was once held by purely nationalistic loyalties.

And the consequences are the same. "Our Side" (whatever that side happens to be) and "Our Guy" (whoever that happens to be) are often viewed through a glass of confirmation bias, such that they really can do no wrong, no matter how wrong they are. Political affiliations, like religious ones, are frequently foundational and once a commitment is made, it is very difficult to shift, without turning our entire world view upside down.

Thus, inevitably, when such institutions or the people that embody them, are attacked, undermined, or corrupted, either physically, psychologically, or through supernatural means — when we are forced to acknowledge that they are not what we have always believed them to be — the result is frequently a profound sense of disconnection. As with our religious faith, when we invest our faith in our state, or our political party, or in some political leader, only to discover that they are not who we thought, or what we thought, the consequences can be world-shattering.

And, of course, terrifying.

Fear of Family Figures or Institutions Being Attacked or Corrupted
We move down the list, from Religion, to State, to Family.

Of course, there are a great many dysfunctional families, which may present a partially or even a completely normal aspect to the outside world, while concealing behind closed doors almost any degree of emotional, physical, or sexual abuse. Such family dysfunction, of course, is at the heart of the Sense of Dread. Parents who should love, nurture, and protect instead harm, exploit and undermine — or even kill. Children who should be loving and responsive to affection sometimes lack basic empathy, and exhibit sociopathic or even psychotic behavior from early childhood.

Again, the revelation of Family Figures and the very Institution of Family being revealed as something other than what we expect it to be, want it to be, need it to be, is profoundly disturbing. Most especially, when a Parent or a Child, who we have always believed to be loving and caring, suddenly changes or is revealed to be someone other than we have always believed — again we stare into the heart of Dread.

Fear of Traditional Celebrations Undermined
We celebrate many of the critical and transitional events of our lives. Beyond that, there are yearly celebrations, some religious, some patriotic or ethnic, that mark the passing of the years. Such celebrations are the hallmarks by which we measure the passing

generations, times when friends and families gather, times for joy and for remembrance.

Of course, family celebrations can also be times of great tension and conflict, where old wounds are uncovered and new ones are inflicted.

But from the perspective of horror, such celebrations have always provided limitless fodder for Dread. Any Celebration where we traditionally come together in happiness and joy, by its very nature, were it to be suddenly and unexpectedly shattered by violence, by death, or by the supernatural, that contrast will inevitably be particularly horrifying.

We expect death, bloodshed, violence, ghosts, and demons to appear at a graveyard at midnight, or in a dark dripping basement, but when those things show up at a child's birthday party, or at a wedding, at a Thanksgiving Celebration, or at Prom Night, the horror is multiplied because the darkness has intruded into a realm of light.

Fear of Intimate Places or Acts Intruded Upon/Violated

As in our discussion of Home Invasion, there are not only places, such as bedrooms and bathrooms, that we consider to be, in a sense, sacred, places where we expect to be safe and protected from intrusion or observation by strangers, it inevitably follows that there are activities that we inevitably expect to be "safe" from observation or intrusion.

Chief among these, of course, are undressing, nudity, sexual activities, bathing and, in Western Societies, toilet activities. It's worth noting that there are cultures where urinating and defecating don't carry the same rigid taboos that they do in Western societies. This is a learned behavior.

In any case, because we expect privacy for these activities, and thus expect that the places in which we carry them out to be private and protected, any unexpected intrusion upon those places and especially upon those acts, is always an effective basis for a frightening sequence.

It's no surprise that we find many film scenes where victims are menaced in the shower, in the bathtub, in bed, while partially or completely undressed, in the midst of sexual activity, or even while sitting on the toilet.

Of course, couples who dare to go out on a date in a horror movie often take their lives into their hands. From the perspective of the Horror Movie, the Date is a "two-for-one," in that it's one of those traditional rituals that we've all been part of — and thus having violence intrude upon it is particularly horrifying.

Also because such scenes involve some sexual element and thus, we also have death, violence, or the supernatural intrude upon the intimacy of the sexual act (even if it's no more than a couple making out in a car before they're found by some deadly menace), thus making the whole thing that much more disturbing.It's worth noting (and others, of course, have made this connection before), that many of the above situations are not only ripe for Horror, but equally ripe for Comedy. The connection between Horror intruding upon the Forbidden and Comedy doing the same warrants much more attention than we can devote to it here.

Fear of Spiritual Contagion

This is the notion that evil may be passed from one person to another, one generation to another, or may infect a particular place, a house for instance, or a patch of ground, a forest, or even a family or a bloodline. Spiritual Contagion lies at the heart of the notion of Curses which may follow a particular person, or even move from one generation to the next, or follow someone or infect those who are close to them, pass from Father to Son, or First Born to First Born. Or it might infect a patch of ground or a sacred, forbidden area or object, such that those who enter into it or touch it might be struck down in some way (thus the Curse of King Tut's Tomb, or the Ark of the Covenant).

The notion of Spiritual Contagion is interesting because, though it obviously carries with it the notion of agency — that some person, or divine or malignant force, is responsible for it — it nevertheless often acts in much the same way as a disease or natural force might act, spreading as a disease might spread, or acting as a poison might.

There is even some overlap here with the concept of Possession, with the notion of the Demon or Incubus, once driven out of the victim, being able thereafter to infect or possess some other person unless dealt with appropriately.

Fear of Wholesale Collapse of Society/Law and Order
We live in the Developed World in a highly advanced, intricately interdependent technological Culture. All of this depends on countless pieces working more-or-less flawlessly all the time. Food, water, sanitation, power, transportation, industry, medicine, information, government: somehow or other, without any single guiding hand, they all seem to integrate reasonably well and it all works.

That is, most of us most of the time can get up in the morning expecting the world around us to function. The lights will turn on when we flick the switch. Water will flow when we turn the faucet and our toilets will work when we flush them. We'll have food on our shelves and garbage trucks to take away the waste. Most of us have jobs and cars or trains that will take us there and home again — and there will be houses or apartments for us to live in.

The overwhelming majority of us will make it home without

being robbed or killed. Neither we nor our loved ones are likely to die or be killed in the near future due to some malevolent act or due to some terrible injury or sickness. Nor will we be dragged from our homes and enslaved.

That's far better than most people could have said about their lives for the majority of human history. It all just seems natural and inevitable for so many of us, all the pieces fitting together and working the way they do.

And yet, those myriad pieces that make up our complex modern technological society are quite delicately balanced, and it wouldn't take much at all for all of those pieces to come apart.

Just as we depend upon our religious institutions, our governments, our families, at the most basic level, we expect our societies as a whole to hold together — for the lights to work, clean water to flow, for there to be food at the grocery store, police on the streets to keep order, for our money to have value, and our basic institutions to keep on working.

And yet we know that in the face of various pressures from within and without, societies have collapsed, leading to wholesale starvation, plague, civil war, genocide, and cannibalism.

But surely, such things could never happen here. That's always what they say before the axe falls. And stories of the Collapse of Civilization, of the End Times, are as old as literature. In the history of motion pictures, the subject of the end of the world was being explored as early as 1916, in a Danish film directed by August Blom aptly entitled *The End of the World*.

Historically, many of these movies have veered more in the direction of adventure or melodrama rather than horror, until George Romero's breakthrough horror movie *Night of the Living Dead* in 1968, and his two follow-ups *Dawn of the Dead* in 1978 and *Day of the Dead* in 1985. These films formed the foundation of an entirely new post-apocalyptic horror sub-genre, which emerged pretty much fully formed from the minds of George Romero and his co-writer Joe Russo.

From these relatively humble beginnings, literally dozens of movies and television series have emerged, all derived, to a greater or lesser extent, from the template laid down by these movies. And while there are many other elements within them that exploit the Sense of Dread, the exploration of the collapse of Law and Order, and everything that we associate with Civil Society and civilization, is very much at the heart of Romero's zombie movies.

URBAN LEGENDS

While "Urban Legends" as such have been around since time immemorial, the term and its broadly understood meaning — that of contagious narratives with a humorous, horrifying, supernatural, or mysterious quality, intended to be taken as true and whose source is usually ascribed to "a friend of a friend" — dates back approximately to 1968, when it was used by folklorist Richard Dorson.

In subsequent decades, Jan Harold Brunvand, a Professor of English at the University of Utah, introduced the concept to the general public in a series of books, *The Vanishing Hitchhiker* (1981), *The Choking Doberman* (1984), *The Mexican Pet: New Urban Legends* (1986) and others.

And yes, there was a horror movie named *Urban Legend,* released in 1998, directed by Jamie Blanks, about a series of mysterious killings related to — well, Urban Legends.

Of course, not all Urban Legends are frightening. Some are comical, such as the "Jato car" — an account in which some misguided soul straps a Jet-Assisted-Take-Off Rocket to the back of his car with unfortunate (if unsurprising) consequences.

Some are bizarre, such as the account of the scuba diver

picked up by a fire-fighting helicopter's water-bombing scoop and dumped high in a tree.

Some Urban Legends simply spread because of wish fulfilment or because people like to be in possession of supposedly secret or special knowledge — thus, the notion that the Proctor & Gamble Logo identifies its relationship to Satanisn, or that secret clues indicate that Paul McCartney of the Beatles (who is alive and well as of this writing) actually died in 1966, or that Elvis (who actually died in 1977) is still alive and in hiding.

These Urban Legends may be odd, amusing, luridly thrilling, or even vaguely sinister, but they're not frightening.

But there is a whole category of such Legends that are intended to raise our hackles, and we'll take some time here to examine a number of them, to see just how these tales draw upon the Sense of Dread as we have explored it in the Chapters above, to create their own unique frisson.

Have You Checked the Children

A teenaged Babysitter downstairs. Two young children asleep upstairs. Then the phone rings. A sinister Voice asks, "Have you checked the Children?" Afraid, she goes upstairs to check. The children are fine.

Later, the phone rings again. The same Voice, the same question. "Have you checked the Children?" Angry, she hangs up.

But the calls keep coming. Eventually, she calls the Police and she's told that they will monitor her phone. If the Man calls again, they'll trace the call and find him. The phone rings once again — "Have you checked the Children?" The frightened Babysitter slams the phone down.

A few seconds later, the phone rings again. She grabs up the phone, only to hear the Police on the other side, "We're on our way! Get out now! The call is coming from inside the house!"

Terrified, the Babysitter rushes from the house, meeting the Police outside. By the time they enter, they find the children inside, having been murdered by the grinning Prowler whom they catch, lurking upstairs in the dark.

There are other, more benign endings to this story, in which the prowler is caught before the children are harmed, or in which the calls turn out to be a hoax perpetrated by one of the children.

There is also an interesting variant in which the Babysitter keeps visiting the children's room, finding them asleep and apparently untouched, but notices a large, life-sized clown statue in the room each time she goes to check. Instead of the Police, she calls the Parents, who proceed to comfort her — until she mentions seeing the clown statue in the children's room, at which point the alarmed mother tells her that there *isn't* any clown statue in the children's room!

The Elements of Dread: We can see quite clearly that this Urban Legend hits on a number of points. Children are endangered. The Young Girl is endangered. The House and the children's bedroom, traditionally places of safety, are threatened and ultimately penetrated. This is rendered especially effective when the Unseen Menace (and this quality of the Menace being Unseen is itself particularly terrifying) which our Protagonist imagines to be outside, actually turns out to be within the apparently Safe Space of the house itself.

The above Urban Legend was the basis of the 1979 feature, *When a Stranger Calls,* directed by Fred Walton, as well as its 1993 sequel and 2006 remake.

The Hook
This story, or variants of it, dates back at least as far as the 1950s.

A Couple is parked in an isolated Lover's Lane, going about the sorts of things that couples do in Lover's Lanes, when the music on the radio is interrupted by a special News Report.

A Maniac has escaped from a nearby Asylum for the Criminally Insane. He can be immediately identified because he has a missing hand, replaced by a *Hook*. He is violent and extremely dangerous. The Girl is frightened and wants to leave, but her Boyfriend, of course, would much rather stay and continue their previous activities.

Unfortunately, the mood's been broken and finally, after repeated requests, the annoyed and frustrated Boyfriend starts the car and peels out of Lover's Lane.

He drives back in angry silence, pulls up to her home, gets out of the car and circles around to open her door. As he does, he freezes in shock.

A *HOOK* is hanging off of the Passenger Side door.

As with most Urban Legends, there are many variations on this story, some involving hooks, some not.

One popular version places the same couple in the same isolated Lover's Lane, the same music interrupted by the same urgent news report about the Escaped Maniac (sans the identifying Hook).

In this variant, the Couple continues their amorous activities until the Young Girl pauses, believing that she hears someone or "something" in the surrounding woods. Perhaps they should go? The Boyfriend, growing frustrated, opts to demonstrate that there's no one out there and departs, leaving his Girl behind, locked in the car.

Time passes and there's no sign of the departed Boyfriend — only the Young Girl begins to hear a strange sound, the sound of something scraping rhythmically across the roof of the car — shff-shff, shff-shff, shff-shff. Over and over. But what could it be? A branch, blowing in the wind? But there wasn't any branch low enough to touch the car when they drove up.

And where has her Boyfriend gone? She realizes that he's taken the car keys with him. There's no way to escape and she's too terrified to leave the car.

Finally, morning comes, and the Police arrive. They knock on the window and she sees horror in their faces as she opens the car door. As they start to take her out of the car, one of the Officers warns her — whatever she does, she must *not* look back toward the car.

But as they lead her away, her curiosity gets the better of her and she turns back to look.

Her Boyfriend has been hanged from a tree directly above the car. As the wind moves the body back and forth, the tips of his shoes brush the top of the car — "shff-shff, shff-shff."

The Elements of Dread: Here we have an intrusion upon a protected activity, in this case sexual activity. While a car isn't exactly the same as a home or a bedroom, it often acts as a surrogate, a home away from home, in this case a place that young couples can go and find privacy for intimate contact. Of course, it's often portrayed as a place where such contact is interrupted in various horrifying ways. In the latter version, the Young Girl is left alone, vulnerable, and under threat. The further element of insanity, in the form of the Mad Killer, and deformity, in the form of the hooked hand, are also present.

There is also, in both versions, the revelation of the unexpected closeness to Death, in the former when the hook on the door is revealed, in the latter, when the unfortunate Young Girl turns back and realizes that the mysterious sound was due to her own Boyfriend's body brushing against the roof of the car mere inches above her head.

The Licked Hand

A Young Girl is being left home alone for the first time, but is comforted as her beloved dog is there to protect her. That night, she hears a news broadcast warning of a killer loose in the neighborhood. Terrified, she proceeds to check all of the doors and windows, making sure that they're locked (but forgetting to check the basement), and then takes the dog with her and heads to bed.

Later that night, she awakens in darkness to the sound of something dripping in the nearby bathroom, but she's too afraid to get out of bed to check. She reaches her hand down and is met by the sensation of her dog licking her hand. She returns to a restless sleep, waking every so often, always to the sound of that odd dripping coming from the bathroom, and each time she reaches her hand down and is reassured by the lick from her dog.

Finally, morning comes, and in the light of day she rises, no longer afraid, and goes to the bathroom. There, she discovers the horrifying source of the dripping — her dog is hanging there, his throat cut, his blood slowly dripping onto the floor — and on the bathroom mirror is scrawled in blood, "Humans can lick too. . . ."

Variations have the parents arriving home, discovering the killer under the bed, or in a closet, or the parents killed, or the daughter.

The Elements of Dread: Again, there is intrusion into a Safe Space, into the house, into the bedroom, under the bed, and into the bathroom. A child is menaced, a dog is killed. There is blood and also the revelation of intimate and perverse pseudo-sexual contact, in the form of a dangerous and murderous intruder licking a young girl's hand, with all of its queasy suggestiveness.

The Spider Bite

A Young Woman from the Midwest is on vacation in Mexico, and one day she's sunbathing outside her hotel and she feels something crawling on her face — and then a sharp sting. She quickly brushes it away, only to see the remains of a nasty, long-legged *spider* which has just bitten her on the cheek.

Later, when she returns home, she notices that there's a tiny red spot there, marking the spot where the spider has bitten her. At first, it's only slightly annoying. She puts a drop of antiseptic on it and tries to forget about it.

But she can't. It grows progressively worse, swelling, and becoming more itchy and painful as the days pass, until finally her whole cheek appears to be red and swollen. She goes to the Doctor, who suggests that the bite must have become infected and gives her some antibiotics to take.

But the wound continues to get worse, continues to swell, and the itching becomes unbearable.

Finally, one night, the wound *pops* — and thousands of baby spiders proceed to pour out, scurrying across the terrified Woman's face!

Variations place the home of the Woman in various Eastern cities, sometimes in the U.S. or in England, the place that she visits varies also. Sometimes it's in South or Central American locales, or sometimes even in the Southern United States. Also, sometimes the spider's bite is on the Woman's head, with the spiders growing and hatching within the Woman's hair.

The Elements of Dread: Obviously, first and foremost, this legend takes advantage of our fear of spiders. There's a Woman in danger. Also, the notion of bodily contamination, of foreign living things growing within us. And it also touches on the idea of the fear of foreign and potentially sinister places, touching on the broadly held racist idea that somehow places "down south" are inherently scary, possibly dirty, and likely to contain hidden dangers.

The Mexican Pet
A Young Couple is vacationing in Mexico by the beach, and one day the Wife discovers a small, bedraggled stray puppy trembling against the wall outside the verandah of their motel room. The Wife, feeling sorry for the little creature, puts out some food and water for it and, after a few days, allows it to come into their room and sleep with them. By the end of their vacation, she's fallen in love with the tiny creature, who is now sharing their bed and snuggling with her, licking her face and taking tiny bits of food from her fingers.

Having fallen in love with it, she decides that they can't possibly leave it behind, and so when they travel back home, they take their new pet with them, the Wife holding it wrapped in a warm blanket.

Once back in the States, they decide to take their new doggie to the Vet, so that it can get checked out and get its shots. As soon as the Vet takes a look at their new puppy, he recoils in horror.

"This isn't a dog!" he says. "It's a dock rat!"

The Elements of Dread: Just as spiders take center stage in the "Spider Bite" Urban Legend, we have the Rat taking center stage in this one. Again, an inherent object of loathing manages to work its way into safe spaces, a bedroom and a bed. We have the element of contamination, as the vermin touches, snuggles with, and licks the Woman. And of course, the central object of the creature's "affection" is a Woman, traditionally thought of as more vulnerable. In addition, there is the notion of concealment, of something horrible hiding beneath the surface of that which we perceive as friendly, affectionate, and loving — a puppy.

The Vanishing Hitchhiker
It's late at night and a light rain is falling as a tired Motorist drives

down a deserted road on an open stretch of rural country. As he rounds a treacherous curve in the road, his headlights catch sight of a forlorn Young Girl standing by the side of the road, her thumb outstretched.He pulls over to let the girl in.

"Sorry," he says, "the front seat is full of junk. Hope you don't mind climbing into the back." The Young Girl doesn't mind and clambers into the back seat. The Man notices that she's pale and shaking from the cold, and offers her his coat to keep warm. She asks him if he might drive her to her home, giving him an address a few miles further on down the road. He agrees.

As they drive, the Man asks her how she came to be out in the rain on the side of the road, but the only answer she gives is that she's " . . . trying to get home."

After a short time, the Man spots the house off the side of the road described by the Young Girl and pulls the car over. As he turns around to bid the Girl good-bye, he's met by a sudden shock.

The car is empty. There's no sign of the Young Girl. Not only has she vanished without a trace, the coat that he lent to her is gone as well. Not sure at first what to do, the Man finally goes to the house and knocks on the door.

The door is opened by an Elderly Man and his Wife. As he starts to explain what happened, they interrupt him. In fact, they've been expecting him. The Young Girl, they tell him, was their daughter. It seems that she died in a tragic accident, trying to hitchhike home on that treacherous curve, and ever since, on the Anniversary of her Death, she shows up on that road and tries to get home.

She's been trying to get home every year since her death — over forty years ago. They buried her in that cemetery, they say, pointing to a nearby graveyard. The grave is just inside the gate.

Still not quite believing what he's been told, the Man heads to the Cemetery and passes through the gate. There, in the place the Old Couple described, was the grave of the Young Girl — with his coat draped across it.

The Elements of Dread: The Sense of Dread encompassed by the Vanishing Hitchhiker Legend is much more subtle than in the previous legends. No rats. No spiders. No maniacs. No real sense of danger at all. Yet we find it chilling. Once again, we have the setting of the car, the protected space, the home-away-from-home surrogate. The Driver allows someone into that safe space, a Young Girl apparently in need — again the *appearance* of helplessness — only to have it revealed at the end that what seemed to be normal and helpless is actually something very different. He has welcomed something in that is Dead, a Restless Spirit that wanders away from her grave. And while this particular spirit seems more tragic than malevolent, the mere notion of coming close to such a being brings with it a deep disquiet — it awakens our Sense of Dread.

EXERCISES ····································

- Make a List of your Favorite Horror Movies and write out which specific Elements of Dread each one uses in order to produce its scares.
- Write two scenes for a possible horror movie, each one drawing on and developing different Elements of Dread as discussed above. Note: each scene may use more than one Element of Dread.
- Find a Scary Urban Legend not described above and work out which Elements of Dread it contains.

4
THE TOOLBOX
OF DREAD

The oldest and strongest emotion of mankind is fear, and the
oldest and strongest kind of fear is fear of the unknown.

H.P. Lovecraft

We've spent a lot of time examining the biological, psychological
and cultural basis for the emotion of fear — the basis for our experience of Dread.

Now we're going to see if we can figure out how to write a
screenplay that scares the hell out of the reader, and will ultimately
scare the hell out of the viewer.

That, of course, is always the objective, to create, for the reader,
the experience a viewer will have watching the movie.

To do that, it's important to understand some things that are
essential in crafting any story.

Emotions never just "happen" in any story. Whatever the emotion may be, we don't laugh, we don't cry, we aren't sad, or afraid,
or filled with joy, simply because "things happen" on screen.

Nothing "just happens" on screen — or on the page. Everything
is a decision made by the writer or by the director (or, of course, by
the actor). The decisions that we make become the emotions that
our readers, and, ultimately, our viewers experience.

If a scene isn't scary, but should be, or isn't touching, but should be, or isn't exciting, but should be, it's because somebody has made a wrong decision. Something is missing that should be present. Somebody — and it may be you — has got some work to do.

Never assume that because an emotion "ought" to be present at a certain point in your story that it will somehow appear automatically. Surely, you might think, Grandma's just died, so obviously, everyone should be sad right about now, both in the scene and, of course, in the audience.

But the harsh reality is that we've seen lots of scenes like this, and sometimes they pull on our heart strings and sometimes they just come across as phony or as nothing at all. The characters on the screen, or on the page, may be crying — but we're not.

And, of course, it works the same with scares. The characters may be terrified by the pursuing horror — but we are not. We've seen it all before. We don't relate to it. We don't experience their fear.

That is always the challenge: to make the reader, and by extension the viewer, experience the emotion that the characters within the story are feeling. You can never just assume that because your characters are sad, the reader will be sad or because your characters are terrified your readers will be terrified.

The Second Thing to understand, especially in relation to a surprise twist or a suspenseful sequence or a jump scare or any other surprise moments or sequences that produce an emotional reaction, is this:

THE EMOTIONAL REACTION IS IN THE STRUCTURE, NOT IN THE SURPRISE

On a certain level, this should be obvious. If it weren't true, we wouldn't be able to re-watch a comedy that contains jokes or gags that depend on surprise twists and reversals. If the twist was essential for making us laugh — then the jokes wouldn't be funny a second time.

But they are. We can watch great comedies, knowing exactly what the jokes are going to be, whether it's physical, verbal, or behavioral comedy — and it's still funny.

In exactly the same way, great horror and suspense movies, even when you've seen them multiple times and know exactly when every shock and every jump scare is coming, can be just as effective — just as scary, just as suspenseful — as they were the first time you saw them.

One of the great non-genre examples of this is the concluding sequence of Ron Howard's *Apollo 13* (1995). Pretty much everyone who watches this movie, because it's based on a famous historical event, knows that the Astronauts got home safe. On that basis, there ought to be no suspense involved in their re-entry.

But the filmmakers make the decision, at a certain point just as the re-entry begins, to leave the Astronauts and focus on those who are waiting at home — that was a key *structural* decision. A News broadcast clarifies that they're going into "radio blackout," that blackout has only ever lasted three minutes, and after three minutes, we'll know if they survived re-entry or there will only be — silence.

And then the clock starts to tick down as we move from family members, the Wives, the Children, the elderly Mother, the Son at the Military Academy, the various Members of Mission Control, all watching, all waiting, frozen — the three minutes pass. The emotionless voice keeps calling to *Odyssey*. No answer. No answer. No answer. Silence.

The tension is unbearable — and then, a crackle. On the TV screen, a glimpse of parachutes opening — and Jim Lovell's voice finally comes over the speaker, and instantly, all of the tension is released — everyone explodes!

Including, by the way, everyone who's watching the movie. The tension has been ratcheted so incredibly high that we're cheering too.

Even though, of course, we always knew that they were going to be fine. And no matter how many times we watch the movie, the tension ratchets up just the same, the release is just the same.

That's why you can hear the same joke over and over again and still laugh. That's why you can watch the same scary scene from a great horror movie and be terrified over and over again.

An emotional scene often has the structure of a joke. In fact, such scenes are often called "gags," whether in reference to comedy, to action, to suspense, or to horror. Structurally, there are similarities in scenes that build toward laughter as well as in scenes that build toward terror.

USE OF TENSION

As we mentioned above, any emotion can be intensified through "ratcheting," in which the structure of the scene compels a character or characters to hold in an emotion, and we follow as the contained emotion builds, builds, builds toward some final moment of release.

A wonderful example of this is in the TV Movie directed by John Newland (of *One Step Beyond* fame), *Don't be Afraid of the Dark* (1973).

It features a young housewife (played by Kim Darby) menaced by a host of tiny malevolent creatures that she's accidentally freed from a bricked-up fireplace in her new home.

There is a truly memorable scene in which she's at dinner with her husband and some houseguests. She's already on-edge because of a number of mysterious happenings — hearing sinister voices — all of it dismissed by her impatient husband.

Of course, we've heard the voices. We know that she's freed something horrible that was trapped down in that fireplace, and so we know that something's going to happen.

As the dinner party proceeds, *something* under the table tugs her napkin off her lap. One of her guests gives it back to her. She tries to behave normally, to dismiss it, to ignore what just happened — and yet again, the tension is ratcheted, as that *something* tugs the napkin off a second time.

Then, she looks under the table, only to see one of the nasty little creatures lurking there, staring up at her.

She *screams* — tension is released. But nobody else sees the thing. And, of course, nobody believes her . . . .

For those of us who saw this movie over forty years ago, it remains one of the hallmarks of Nightmare Cinema. Even watching it today, it far surpasses in terms of out-and-out terror, the over-embellished CGI complexities of Troy Nixey's 2010 remake.

One of the best examples of the use of building tension is the opening of George Romero's classic original, *Night of the Living Dead* (1968).

The first fourteen minutes of this movie is an almost continuous ratcheting of tension, from the time that we first spot the sinister figure in the distance, as Barbara and Johnny place the memorial on their father's grave (we, of course, know that something's not right), as Johnny taunts Barbara, "They're coming to get you, Barbara!"

Then, as the loping figure continues to advance, we start to see him more clearly. There's just something a bit odd about him. He's not walking quite right. And his clothes are scuffed-up. Barbara's concern, of course, is that the man might hear him being mocked by Johnny. That is — right up until she's suddenly and viciously attacked! As far as the two of them are concerned, squabbling Brother and Sister a few seconds before, this all comes literally out of nowhere.

Now Johnny intervenes, defending her — only to find himself in a life-and-death struggle as Barbara looks on, shocked. How is this happening? In a matter of seconds, the fight is over. Johnny is either rendered unconscious or killed, and now the Attacker is after her.

She's now running for her life. She falls, kicks off her shoes, makes it back to her car with seconds to spare. But what now? No keys. Johnny had them! Now the Attacker attempts to break into the car, grabs a stone, smashes away at the window.

Finally, as the window breaks and he reaches in, groping for her, she pulls the emergency brake, and the car starts rolling down the hill with the Attacker loping after it.

But the escape is only momentary. The car runs against a tree. Barbara, shoeless, is forced to flee on foot, with the Attacker close behind.

She makes her way across a field, the Fiend in close pursuit, gets to a dark and apparently abandoned farmhouse. She grabs a knife, but what is she to do? The phone? Not working. Outside, night has fallen, and the Lone Attacker has been joined by Others. What is going on?

She climbs the stairs, only to be confronted by a mangled corpse lying at the top of the steps!

Fleeing in terror, she flings the door open, only to find herself staring into blinding headlights — and Ben — the first human being she's seen since losing her brother.

There are very few horror movies of any generation, with an opening as effective as *Night of the Living Dead*. Central to that effectiveness is that it starts with an essentially normal state of affairs, a squabbling Brother and Sister going about their business. It could be anybody — and that is the idea. Since this is an event that is happening across the world, it would, in effect, be happening to Everybody — to Anybody. This is just where we happen to enter into this World-Wide Event. It is because neither of them is special, because Barbara has no special skills, no special understanding of what the Hell is going on, that we relate to her. We relate to her helplessness, to her confusion — and to her terror.

Starting with them rather than, say, starting with Ben, or with any of the other characters who end up trapped in that house, was not a random decision, even though the story ultimately leaves Barbara largely behind. Russo and Romero, who wrote the screenplay, made that decision because they wanted us to experience that initial introduction to the events of the Return of The Dead, through Barbara's eyes — through the eyes of one of the most vulnerable characters in the story.

Because she is helpless and has no idea what is going on, we relate to her terror. And because her fear continues to mount, continues to "ratchet," we become ever more afraid as her confusion, her sense of helplessness, and her terror grows.

BUILD TO THE SCARE, CONTINUE TO BUILD, AND FOLLOW THE RELEASE WITH ANOTHER SCARE

In this scene, as in many other scenes, Romero builds to the scare, as in the opening Graveyard Scene, and then continues to build, allowing new scares to mount. When there is a moment of possible relief, as when Barbara reaches the refuge of the farmhouse, we are then confronted with yet another *jump scare* in the form of the hideous body at the top of the stairs which drives Barbara out, into the arms of Ben outside.

Tension release often comes in the form of a *reversal* — in some surprising or unexpected direction.

A wonderful example of this comes from *The Haunting* (1963), Robert Wise's brilliant version of the Shirley Jackson novel.

A group of diverse Ghost Hunters has taken up residence in Hill House, hoping to penetrate the secrets of the Other World. What haunts Hill House? No one can really be sure as the nameless entity never actually shows itself, appearing instead as a terrifying thumping, moving invisibly down the hall beyond the doors, a rattling at a doorknob, a vast pressure that bows a door in almost to the point of shattering. . . .

And in one specific scene, two of the occupants, the neurotically vulnerable Eleanor, and Theodora, the sophisticated lesbian psychic, are now sharing a room (and a bed) after the terrifying events of the previous night.

Eleanor wakes in the shadowed darkness to the sounds of muffled voices. She whispers to Theo not to speak, lest whoever or whatever it is realizes that she's in her room. She reaches out her hand, whispers for Theo to take it.

Eleanor stares at the wall, at a curled pattern of leaves in the plaster. Or is it? Because as the voices continue, a Man's voice mumbling, a Woman's laughing, it seems as if the simulacrum of a face appears in the molded shapes of the plaster.

Meanwhile, the sound of a child's voice, crying in torment, is added to the others. Eleanor feels Theo clutching her hand, tighter and tighter. The sounds grow more insistent — Eleanor grows more and more horrified. Theo's hand is almost crushing hers.

We hear Eleanor in Voice Over, "If there's one thing I cannot stand it is for anyone to hurt a child." She goes on, "I will get my mouth to open and I will yell, I will yell, I will yell!"

Finally, she breaks the spell and screams, "STOP IT!"

As she does, the light flips on. Far across the room, Theo sits up in bed. Eleanor has been asleep on a settee.

"What is it, Eleanor? What's wrong?"

It's only then that Eleanor sits up, stands, lifting her hand, in cold shock.

"God," she says, "Who's hand was I holding?"

Of course, the finesse of the scene, as it's conceived and ultimately shot, is that we never see Theo until the final reveal, and yet, because of the way that it's structured, remaining always either tight on Eleanor or on the exceptionally creepy plaster pattern on the wall, that we never even think about the fact that Theo remains unseen during the whole of the scene, right up until that reveal.

Inevitably, one of the advantages of developing a script with the Director who's going to be shooting it is that both Screenwriter (in this case, Nelson Gidding) and Director already know how scenes like these are going to be shot.

It will always be a challenge in writing a Spec script when trying to craft a scene like this, when you alone understand that it must be seen on screen in a certain way in order for a critical reveal to work. It's one of those situations that requires a certain finesse in describing it.

On the one hand, you never want to be accused of "directing on the page." On the other hand, the goal is always to try to create, in the mind of the reader, the experience that a viewer would have, while watching the finished film.

FAKE TENSION BREAK

There are any number of versions of this, often included in a "curiously afraid" sequence. That is, a scene in which some character is being drawn down that alley or down that flight of basement stairs or down that shadowed corridor where we all know (including that character) that they really shouldn't go.

It's common to interrupt that journey with a Fake Tension Break. The cat in the alley knocks over a garbage can, or the Hero turns on the stairs and sees their reflection in a dusty mirror. The result is a *Jump Scare* — we think that it's *something* — but no, it's nothing.

Those beats produce a *Tension Break*. The character goes "phew ...," and we do the same. But then, they keep on going down the stairs, down the corridor, down the alley — allowing the tension toward the final reveal to continue to build.

Instead of actually relieving tension, the Fake Tension Break actually places us more on edge. It acts as a preview of the real terror that we know (though they may not) is coming.

THE TWIST

In the same way that the laugh in a gag comes from a sudden unexpected twist or reveal at the end of the gag, so in the case of a horror gag — the resolution often comes in the form of a sudden and unexpected reveal that elevates our sense of horror, that "pays off" the gag.

As with a comedic gag, the twist, the surprise reveal, should be set up in some way. We don't see it coming, but in retrospect, the groundwork was established.

The resolution of the scene in *The Haunting* is a great example of this; on the one hand, the reveal of Theo being across the room and thus of Eleanor having been holding the hand of "something else" is a fantastic twist. But it was fairly set up — because we went through the entire scene without seeing or hearing a word from Theo. If Theo had actually been next to Eleanor, really holding her hand, wouldn't we have expected the camera to cut to her, to show her reaction? Yes, in retrospect. And yet, the way in which the scene is staged and shot, fortunately, doesn't even make us ask ourselves that question.

Another fantastic example of this is the ultimate twist ending of Alejandro Amenábar's *The Others* (2001), in which the "ghosts" haunting the isolated country home of the high-strung Grace and her light-sensitive children during World War II are ultimately revealed to actually be the new *living* occupants of the house. It is Grace and her children who are finally revealed to be the Ghosts, unaware of their lifeless state until forced to realize the truth.

Yet, this surprise twist is properly set up, especially when Grace's husband, who disappeared in World War II and was long thought dead, arrives home unexpectedly for a brief stay, only to depart as mysteriously as he arrived. But from where, after all, has he come, long after the war's end? And where does he go and why? It may almost have been too much of a hint — but even so, it doesn't keep the ending, when it finally comes, from being exceptionally chilling.

THE JUMP SCARE

We spoke at length about the startle response, and Horror Movies have taken advantage of this from the earliest days of cinema.

This was more of a challenge during the era of silent motion pictures, but even then, there are memorable uses of the Jump Scare.

One of the most notable among these is the shocking reveal of the scarred face of Lon Chaney's Phantom, in Rupert Julian's *Phantom of the Opera* (1925).

Also, we can't leave out one of the most shocking images in all of cinematic history, featured in Luis Buñuel's Surrealist short, *Un Chien Andalou* (1929).

It features a scene in which a man lifts a straight razor to a woman's eye, starts to draw it. The image then cuts to a shot of a narrow cloud sliding across the moon, and we are, in a sense, comforted, believing that the visual metaphor is going to substitute for the ghastly reality. Then we cut back to the continuation of the image — a terrifying Jump Scare as the blade literally slices the woman's eye open — an image of graphic horror unmatched for generations.

In the decades that followed, after the advent of sound, the uses of the Jump Scare increased, although it wasn't used as frequently as one might imagine.

Notably, it cropped up in Jacques Tourneur's *The Cat People* (1942), in which the character Jane Randolph, walking down a lonely street at night can hear the echoing clatter of an unseen woman's heels following behind her — and then they stop. Nervous, she keeps walking. But somehow, she senses that she's still being followed — by something.

Then just as she hears what might be the snarl of a leopard, there's a loud *hiss!* It's the air brakes of a bus as it pulls to a stop in front of her. Rescue.

An even more memorable Jump Scare shows up in Christian Nyby's *The Thing from Another World* (1951), rumored to have actually been directed by Howard Hawks, by the way, in which the previously unseen Thing has been trapped in the greenhouse at the Polar Station where the action of the story takes place. The Military Men, armed to the teeth, led by the no-nonsense Captain Hendry, approach the heavy door. They're ready to enter and face the Thing.

Hendry gives the order for the door to be opened — only to find the Thing standing right in the doorway, facing them! Chaos — and gunfire — ensues.

Moving through into the sixties and seventies, filmmakers got the hang of using jump scares. Finally, in the eighties, they'd pretty much figured out how to do it; most notably they'd realized that accompanying a visual Jump Scare with some loud noise, whether justified or not, amplified the effect significantly.

Since then, it's become Standard Operating Procedure.

DIFFERENT KINDS OF JUMP SCARES

The Sudden Jump Scare

Characters are simply going about their business, whatever it might be, when, out of nowhere . . . .

Well, here are two examples — both sharks.

First: Stephen Spielberg's *Jaws* (1975). They're out on the boat. Quint is working on his fishing reel, Hooper is "driving the boat," and Chief Brody is starting another chum line, and as he starts to toss out this nasty mix of stinking dead fish and blood he begins to complain. Why can't Hooper take this messy job for a change — as he promptly tosses a load of chum into the gaping jaws of the gigantic white shark, rising to the bait. (The tension of this Jump Scare, of course, is released by one of the best lines of the movie, "We're gonna need a bigger boat. . . . "

Second: Renny Harlin's *Deep Blue Sea* (1999). The Team of shark experts is trapped in an underwater moon pool, and are fighting amongst themselves because the super-intelligent shark breeding experiment has gone a bit off the rails, and Randall, played by Samuel L. Jackson, proceeds to give the others a serious dressing down about how they all need to stick together and find a way out — at which point a gigantic shark jumps out of the moon pool, grabs him, and drags him to his death while the others look on in horror.

Now, let's be clear. *Deep Blue Sea* is a very silly movie, but it does contain that one very effective Jump Scare.

"Jump Scares" That Relieve Tension in a Mounting Suspense Scene

David Robert Mitchell's *It Follows* (2014) has a prime example of this when Protagonist Jay, having inherited the "curse" after having sex with her boyfriend and finding herself relentlessly pursued by the Lethal Demon of the title, who is invisible to everyone but those who have been cursed (and, of course, us), finds herself on the beach with several of her friends — when the relentless "It" shows up, approaching her in the form of a Young Girl.

When she finds herself grabbed by the hair and lifted, she pulls lose, and she and the others retreat in terror to a shack on the beach. Her friends still don't know quite what's happening, even when she empties a revolver at the approaching menace, to no effect.

Fred, one of her friends left outside and in the line of fire, shouts for her to stop shooting as the Demon rises, unhurt by the bullets. Jay frantically locks the door, only to glimpse a large form moving past a narrow window, then something starts pounding on the door.

And then the Jump Scare — as "It" smashes a big hole down low, toward the bottom of the door, sending splinters flying across the room and then . . . silence.

A brief moment of relief follows as, for a few beats, nothing happens, but surely it can't be over. As we MOVE IN on the hole low down on the door, suddenly — Fred sticks his head into view — another Jump — as he demands to know what's going on. There isn't anybody out here! Again, the tension is briefly relieved as he rises, moves away.

And then, once again another Jump Scare — as the Demon appears in one of its truly terrifying forms (of which there are many), grey-faced, black-eyed, crawling in through the hole

— sending Jay rushing out through the back.

Mitchell manages to accomplish something else in this scene which is also a variation on a standard Jump Scare. That is —

Ending a Scene with a Second Larger Jump Scare
after an Earlier Jump Scare
All of this goes back to the notion of ratcheting up the tension in the scene, and using successive scares followed by tension release and then continuing to build.

One of the best examples of this can be found in James Wan's *The Conjuring* (2013), in the sequence that begins with Carolyn Perron in her daughter's room upstairs — there's a sudden huge *crash*! We all Jump!

That Jump Scare brings her to the top of the stairs. All of the pictures hanging on the wall down the stairwell have fallen. Heading down and searching the first floor of her new home, she begins to hear the mysterious clapping, part of the hide-and-clap game that we've seen her play earlier with her children. Only her children are all upstairs — so who's clapping?

And then, as she circles through the darkened rooms of the first floor, she hears the sound of a door opening. She turns, and sees that it's the door to the basement. The sound of someone playing the broken piano comes up from below. She takes a step down, turns on the light, shouts that she's going to lock up whoever it is down there!

And then the next Jump Scare, as the basement door *slams* into her face, sending her careening head-over-heels down the basement steps, trapping her there. She rises, bruised, half-stunned — and terrified.

The basement itself is full of junk, full of shadows, lit only by the light from a single incandescent bulb.

She stares this way and that — and then, out of a dark space across the basement, a child's ball comes flying out, bouncing across the floor toward her.

She breaks, rushing back to the stairs. As she does, another Jump Scare as the lone bulb *bursts*, leaving her and the whole basement, in total darkness. For a moment, all we can hear are the sounds of her desperate scramble on the stairs — and the sounds of a child's laughter, then her fumbling with matches.

Finally, as she lights a match with a trembling hand, she comes back into view. She leans forward, trying to penetrate the darkness below. One match burns out. She lights another, continuing to stare *downward*, and thus directing our attention in that direction, seeing nothing.

Then, a child's voice, "Do you want to play hide and clap?" — and the Final Jump Scare as hands emerge from the darkness behind and above her, clapping.

For the remainder of the Standard Jump Scare Types referred to below, we'll generally leave it to you to come up with examples of your own. They are so common that they can be found in countless Horror Films.

AUDIBLE JUMP SCARES

These range from the classic "over-amplified phone ring" to the sudden crash of thunder, to a sudden off-screen scream or the howl of a cat or, well — you no doubt have your own examples.

Loud noises trigger our startle reflex. If we're already in a state of tension, this works even better. It didn't take filmmakers long to figure this out and exploit it.

A Loud Noise will make the audience jump.

VISUAL JUMP SCARE

Almost always, Visual Jump Scares are combined with an Audible cue. If it isn't practical to incorporate one into the action itself, then it will simply be added to the music track or just laid into the soundtrack itself — a loud *Sting* or *Blare* to help sell the Jump.

There are countless variations of the Visual Jump Scare. These are general categories, but far from an exhaustive list:

From Off Screen

A hand reaches in from the side, from below, from above. This can be an actual menace, though more often than not, it's a "fake" jump scare.

A Cat, a Dog, comes jumping in, or a bird flies into a nearby window. Sometimes, in a more sinister version, it might be a bat. Again, this only refers to things entering from Off Screen.

Objects falling into Frame — again, more often than not, these are Fake Jump Scares — some innocent object that defuses tension along the way to a bigger scare.

From Within the Screen

A door, a box, a cabinet, a hatch, or something similar is opened or falls open, revealing something shocking — a body or a head or spiders or rats — anything that produces a sense of shock or horror. Again, the reveal could also turn out to be something harmless, thus relieving tension with a Fake Jump Scare.

A Light Source is turned on or moved, revealing the presence of something in the shadows. Again, it might be a body, a Menacing Presence — or it could simply be a mirror or something harmless (thus a Fake Jump Scare).

Objects within the Frame falling, moving, exploding. Pictures fall off walls, objects go flying, burst into flame. Doors and windows slam.

Movement Reveal

There are many variations on this. A Character may move, revealing Someone or Something behind them.

Someone or Something may rise up into view behind a Character (. . . and yes, we all remember that terrifying moment from Scott Derrickson's *Sinister* (2012), when the Demon popped up behind Ellison).

What is particularly effective about the above Movement Reveal Jump Scare is that, generally, one Character within the scene sees the horror, while the other, the one facing away from it, does not.

A Mirror is turned, revealing Something in the reflection.

A Character opens a curtain or blinds, revealing Something on the other side.

The Camera moves to reveal the Jump Scare — sometimes following a Character or moving in relation to that Character to reveal the presence of Something or someone not previously seen.

Note: Generally, you want to do your best to avoid describing camera moves, so if you really feel that it's necessary for the sake of a particular effect, you would tend to describe these in terms of character movement.

THE FUNDAMENTAL JUMP SCARE CHALLENGE

Jump Scares can be used to great effect in horror movies, or they can come across as cheap and second-rate. Either way, because of their basis in human biology, they're going to produce the expected result. They're going to get the audience to jump. That's why filmmakers continue to depend on them.

That is also why they continue to pose a significant challenge to the horror movie screenwriter.

No matter what you do, Jump Scares will simply never be as scary on the page as they are on the screen.

As a biological limitation, there's nothing you can write that will make a Reader jump in the same way as they will when they see and hear the comparable moment on screen.

That means that a screenplay that depends solely on Jump Scares is not going to be as effective as one that depends on integrating those moments more broadly with the Sense of Dread.

It would be like reading a comedy script where we know where and when we are *supposed* to laugh, without ever actually laughing as we read the screenplay.

If you're writing a comedy, you want the reader to laugh, and if you're writing a horror movie, you definitely want to scare your reader.

EXPLICIT VS. NON-EXPLICIT HORROR

The debate between horror films that rely on explicit images of violence and sexuality and more subtle horror films seems to be a perennial one.

On the one hand, you have classic horror films such as Jack Clayton's *The Innocents* (1961), Robert Wise's *The Haunting* (1963), or Alejandro Amenábar's *The Others* (2001) that show almost nothing in the way of explicit imagery.

On the other, you have some of the truly great horror classics that don't shy away from the explicit depiction of violence and bloodshed, most notably, George Romero's *Dead Trilogy*, Toby Hooper's original *Texas Chainsaw Massacre* (1974), or Clive Barker's *Hellraiser* (1987).

There's a certain critique of Horror Movies that suggests that the more subtle and less-explicit Horror Film is somehow inherently superior — that Films that imply the menace and never show anything explicitly (you know, the way movies used to be made "in the old days") make for better movies.

I think that a much broader perspective is needed, irrespective of the genre. There will always be stories that will work more strongly taking an indirect or subtle approach to the material, and in just the same way, there are always going to be stories that will require a more direct approach.

There are going to be Action Movies that will be more or less explicit in their depiction of violence, Romance Movies that will be more or less explicit in their depiction of sexuality, and Horror Movies that will be more or less explicit in their depiction of Visual Horror.

A big part of the question in developing any story dealing with the depiction of violence, of gore, of sexuality, has to do with what effect those images are going to have on the reader, and by extension, on the viewer — especially on the viewer — because reading about blood and gore, reading about explicit violence, is a much less shocking experience than actually seeing it on screen, and that has to be part of the thought process of any screenwriter developing such material.

What purpose, in relation to your story and your Characters, thematically and emotionally, do these images serve? Why are they on screen? And also — when *are* they on screen?

Ultimately, everything that you put on the page, which is destined to be shown on screen, should be thought of not only in terms of moving the story forward (which, of course it should), but also in terms of its emotional effect.

Inevitably, certain images will horrify, will shock, will even potentially disgust the viewer. Of course, audiences differ, and there will be audiences who view horror movies as a kind of endurance test, who want to be challenged by ever-bloodier, gore-laced, and more disgusting images.

When we talk about Exploitation Cinema, this is what we're talking about. Images are being put on the screen solely to create a thrill, an effect, whether it's to shock, or titillate, or gross out the audience.

The Gore Movies of Herschell Gordon Lewis fall into this category.

There are any number of filmmakers (and screenwriters) who've made a living making Exploitation Films down through the years — and obviously, there has always been and always will be an audience for those movies.

If you're into those movies, I'm not going to say that you shouldn't be, but that's not the kind of Horror Movie that we're talking about.

So, what about the use of graphic violence in a movie that's not being used just for exploitation?

How is it best used, and to what purpose?

Let's consider one of the best examples. That would be George Romero's sequel to *Night of the Living Dead*, his *Dawn of the Dead* (1978). This movie was released unrated, due to its explicit violent content and, unlike the original, was also shot in color, making the violence all the more graphic.

For those of us who saw this movie in its initial release back in 1978, *Dawn* was like nothing that had ever been put on the screen before in terms of its graphically realistic depiction of violence. But Romero made some very interesting creative choices in the making of this movie.

First, the movie starts off in the midst of the absolute chaos of that First Night when the Dead have come back. In the first ten minutes or so, we are assaulted with some of the most horrific images of violence that had ever been put on screen up to that time — most notably shots of people's heads being blown off, and several shots of zombies taking bites out of people and tearing the flesh away in full close-up.

What is most interesting about those opening moments of *Dawn of the Dead* is that the movie never gets as graphically violent as this again. The point is — it doesn't have to. We are so shocked, so put on edge by those images right up front that for the rest of the movie, we simply have the sense that just about anything might happen, anything might abruptly come out of nowhere and assault our senses.

And just in case we start to become complacent, Romero will jab us with another shocking image, such as the moment when a zombie is killed by having a screwdriver thrust through his ear, just to remind us that — yes, don't forget — we're in a world where anything horrible might just happen.

Graphic violence, of course, serves other purposes in Horror Cinema. The depiction of blood itself shocks us. Most of us are conditioned to react to it with distress.

Along the same lines, the sudden intrusion of violent death into otherwise comfortable and normal surroundings is likewise profoundly horrifying. That abrupt transformation of person into mere flesh undermines our very sense of *being*.

The use of violent images and sequences are available to the writer and the filmmaker as tools for creating the Sense of Dread.

But there is also a downside to the use of such images. As with any image or sequence designed to produce a powerful emotional effect, the overuse of such material will inevitably lead to desensitization. The law of diminishing returns applies. It's very much like continuously playing music at full volume. At a certain point, it just becomes noise.

John Carpenter's *The Thing* (1982) is one of the most effective examples of the proper modulation of the use of graphic violence. It has some of the most memorably bloody sequences in any major motion picture of that decade, but Carpenter most definitely chooses his moments.

Some of the most memorable images aren't intrinsically threatening; for instance, the discovery of the body of the Norwegian, his blood pouring in twin frozen streams from his wrists, and the moment when Windows takes his own blood sample by slitting himself under his thumbnail with a scalpel.

These "small" horrors punctuate much more disturbing moments — images of the dormant Thing's discovery and autopsy, and the full-scale horror sequences, most notably the one in which Copper, attempting to revive Norris with a defibrillator, ends up getting his arms bitten off — the sequence that ends with the infamous "spider head" transmutation.

The Thing starts slow and builds its scares, both large and small, in a masterful way. At its heart is a growing sense of paranoia, of Men who never quite know who's human.

ISOLATION/CLAUSTROPHOBIA/DISLOCATION

Another element that *The Thing* develops in a very effective way is the sense of isolation, which is critical to the development of the story. From the very beginning, the Antarctic base is cut off from the outside world, unable to communicate with anybody, and as the story progresses, the sense of intruding cold and darkness grows and grows — until there is nothing left but the two survivors (or is there really only one?) waiting for the cold and the dark to claim them.

We are social animals; thus we associate being cut off from the company of other human beings, from the normal social structures of Family and of Community, with a state of deep unease and outright fear.

Horror Movies have exploited this collective fear of Isolation, Claustrophobia, and Dislocation in countless ways:

Trapped in Narrow Spaces
The most obvious example — characters trapped in tight spaces — anything from the Rock Climber trapped by the boulder in Danny Boyle's *127 Hours* (2010), to Laurie trapped in the clothes closet in John Carpenter's *Halloween* (1978), or Jeffrey trapped in Dorothy Vallens' clothes closet in David Lynch's *Blue Velvet* (1986).

Trapped in Caves/Underground/Graves
Again, many examples — Neil Marshall's *The Descent* (2006), Bruce Hunt's *The Cave* (2005), Rodrigo Cortés' *Buried* (2010), Christopher Smith's *Creep* (2004), or Gary Sherman's *Death Line* (1972). Caves, graves, subway tunnels — places of darkness surrounded by earth — they all seem to inspire an essential sense of dread in us.

Trapped In or Underwater
Of course, the sense of the water as being bottomless, holding unseen terrors and secrets for those who swim in it or dive into it — with *Jaws* being the defining example of this. Then, of course, there's Chris Kentis' *Open Water* (2004), with its terrifying sense of the dislocation of wide open spaces. More recently, there's the deep water Lovecraftian horror of William Eubanks' aptly named *Underwater* (2020).

Trapped on a Ship/Lifeboat/Space Ship
Most notable of these is certainly Christopher Smith's *Triangle*
(2009), a movie that falls somewhere between horror, science
fiction, and an exceptionally eerie exploration of the Bermuda
Triangle myth. There's also Alvin Rakoff's *Death Ship* (1980),
Steve Beck's *Ghost Ship* (2002), or Justin Dix's *Blood Vessel* (2019).

As far as movies that take us in the other direction — stories
of characters trapped in space — we have to go back to Edward
L. Cahn's *It! The Terror from Beyond Space* (1958) as the seminal
movie of a team of space explorers pitted against an almost invulnerable Alien Menace on board an isolated spaceship, along with
Mario Bava's stylishly creepy *Planet of the Vampires* (1965). These
two movies were later reconfigured as Ridley Scott's *Alien* (1979)
with its ideas, in turn, more fully explored and developed by James
Cameron in *Aliens* (1986).

For the full-blown "Haunted House in Outer Space" movie, of
course, there's Paul W. S. Anderson's *Event Horizon* (1997) and, in
a similar mode, there's Christian Alvart's *Pandorum* (2009).

Trapped in Familiar Spaces/Home Invasion
This has proven to be among the most effective uses of the Sense of
Dread: the transformation of a familiar and comfortable environment into a prison, a place in which the Protagonists are trapped,
rendered helpless, threatened by forces, either human or inhuman,
over which they have no control.

On the human side we have the whole Home Invasion sub-
genre, which started with William Wyler's *The Desperate Hours*
(1955), a suitably tense thriller, but restrained compared to the
movies that followed. Among them, Sam Peckinpah's *Straw Dogs*
(1971) and J. Lee Thompson's *Cape Fear* (1962), both of them

re-made, as well as Paul Haneke's *Funny Games* (two versions as well — one shot in Austria in 1997, and an American version shot in 2006), and Bryan Bertino's *The Strangers* (2008).

There are, of course, many variations, and many other movies in which Home Invasions play a much more limited role, including John McNaughton's deeply disturbing *Henry: Portrait of a Serial Killer* (1986).

On the supernatural side, we have Tobe Hooper's classic *Poltergeist* (1982), which laid the groundwork for the "conventional" haunted house, as opposed to the more familiar "creepy old" haunted house, in which usually conventional individuals enter or find themselves trapped in an other-worldly house of some kind.

In *Poltergeist,* both the suburban house and its occupants seem essentially normal and identifiable — yet, somehow, from somewhere, a supernatural element has entered and becomes ever more menacing.

Oren Peli's *Paranormal Activity* (2007) follows in the same path, using the "found footage" approach. Seemingly Normal Suburban House, Normal Couple — and a growing sense of an Intruding Force from Beyond.

Of course, there were six *Paranormal Activity* movies in the franchise — which ultimately demonstrates the Law of Diminishing Returns — but the original movie, and even some of the early sequels maintained a suitably high Sense of Dread.

One of the most effective examples of this is *Ghostwatch*, a pseudo-documentary directed by Leslie Manning and aired on Halloween on the BBC in 1992. It was hosted by real-life Television Hosts, and was intended to document the appearance of any supernatural events in the purported "most haunted house in Britain" — a family home plagued by poltergeist experiences.

The contrast between the jokiness and banality of the early part of the show and what happens later, when the ghost (named "Pipes" by one of the children) starts to show himself in the midst of the drab lower-class home, makes for one of the most chilling examples of the use of Dread ever made.

Trapped by Nature

There's overlap here, of course, with Protagonists trapped in or underwater, but there are other natural environments that are often drawn upon to create the emotion of dread.

Of course, we normally think of being trapped by situations that enclose us, that literally "trap" us, in the sense of mines, caves, chasms, crevasses, buildings collapsed by earthquakes, the rising waters of floods, etc. — and there is no shortage of such scenes and sequences in motion pictures.

The mirror image of claustrophobia is agoraphobia, the fear of open spaces. Sometimes that environment can be equally terrifying — broad, empty landscapes that seem at first devoid of life, and yet may hide something unseen and deadly.

There are many motion pictures in which Characters may find themselves trapped in wide-open spaces, as in *Open Water*, mentioned above, or the chilling sequence from Alfred Hitchcock's *North by Northwest* (1959) in which the Hero finds himself pursued by a machine-gun-wielding crop duster in the midst of wide-open fields.

The desert also offers many opportunities for terror, with movies such as S. Craig Zahler's *Bone Tomahawk* (2015), or Wes Craven's *The Hills Have Eyes* (1977) with its inbred family of Mutants.

Finally, we come back to the terror that haunts the forests, that gives us the word "Panic." It is in the deep woods, especially at night, that we confront our most profound, ancient, and atavistic fears. There is something in us that remembers when we were only animals, subject to all of the threats that lurked in the deep woodland shadows — all the things that stalked and hunted and looked upon us as prey.

Among the movies that explore these fears most effectively are Sam Raimi's original *The Evil Dead* (1981), Eduárdo Sanchez and Daniel Myrick's seminal found-footage movie, *The Blair Witch Project* (1999), Jason Zada's tale of the real-life Japanese Suicide Forest, *The Forest* (2016), and Robert Egger's disturbing directorial debut, *The Witch* (2015).

In all of these movies, the environment itself plays a critical part in creating the Sense of Dread.

In addition to Natural Phenomena like storms and floods, there is Darkness, featured in a number of recent movies, as well as perpetual cold or overwhelming heat caused either by Aliens, the Supernatural, or our tampering with the Laws of Nature.

Of course, Nature also rebels, in the form of living things turning against us. Insects, spiders, worms, rats, parasites, normal animals and pets gone mad, et al. — attacking us at their conventional sizes, or mutated and rendered gigantic, have filled motion picture screens.

Trapped inside Our Heads/Mind Control/Possession
One of the deepest fears that emerge from our Sense of Dread is that of losing our selves — control over our bodies, our minds, and our souls. Movies have long explored the notion of hypnotic and psychic Mind Control, going all the way back to the silent days and Robert Weine's Expressionist Masterpiece, *The Cabinet of Dr. Caligari* (1920), and the early sound film Archie Mayo's *Svengali* (1931).

Since that time, the concept has been explored in many films, ranging from Wolf Rilla's *Village of the Damned* (1960), with its host of sinister blonde-haired mind-controlling children, to the cold-war thrills of John Frankenheimer's *The Manchurian Candidate* (1962), all the way up through Ehren Kruger's *Skeleton Key* (2005) to Jordan Peele's *Get Out* (2016).

Movies dealing with Possession have likewise made a significant impact on the horror genre.

One of the most terrifying variations on this theme can be found in Don Siegel's *Invasion of the Body Snatchers* (1956), when Miles and Becky are fleeing from a town whose inhabitants have been completely taken over by the body-snatching pods. Exhausted, unable to sleep (because if they sleep, they will be taken over), Miles goes to see if the coast is clear, leaving Becky in hiding beneath a bridge.

When he returns, he kisses Becky, only to recoil in horror, realizing that he has just kissed something that is no longer human — a thing that no longer has a soul. In the moment that he'd left her, Becky had fallen asleep — and become one of "them."

In all of the canon of fifties science fiction/horror, there are very few moments as terrifying as this one. It shows nothing — except the loss of someone's soul.

In 1973, William Friedkin's ground-breaking *The Exorcist*, based on the novel by William Peter Blatty, laid the groundwork for an entire sub-genre of movies about possession, in much the same way that George Romero's *Night of the Living Dead* did for zombie movies.

Not only that, it also broadly increased the number of people who claimed that they were actually possessed (in the same way that flying saucer sightings increased after the release of Spielberg's *Close Encounters of the Third Kind* in 1977).

An interesting point to make about *The Exorcist*, with its encyclopedic collection of terrors, large and small, is that one of its most terrifying images comes from the brief scene in which Doctors are administering a spinal tap to Regan, and during the procedure, we see a brief spurt of blood coming from her back as the catheter is slid into her. The sense of her suffering, her vulnerability, the suffering of her Mother, creates a real sense of queasy discomfort in the viewer. We are shocked at the sight of the spurting blood—but also deeply disturbed at the suffering that this child is being forced to endure — even though it's a medical procedure.

Possessed Men, Women, Children — even semi-inanimate objects such as dolls or trees have been featured in a variety of movies to varying effects. Often the greatest effect in terms of the Sense of Dread comes from the deep conflict that occurs between what we have come to expect Someone or Something to be, and what they become after being occupied or taken over by *The Other*.

Of course, people can also be possessed by the ghosts of the dead, as in Stuart Rosenberg's *The Amityville Horror* (1979), or inhabited by alien beings as in *The Invasion of the Body Snatchers* or Andrew Niccol's *The Host* (2013).

Inevitably the storyteller, in dealing with the mythology of mind control or possession must find the means to permit there to be balance in the story. That is, if the Antagonist is overwhelmingly powerful, whether that side is the Force of Darkness or an Alien from Beyond, it becomes difficult to properly structure any kind of real defense, and thus a real story where we believe that victory of any kind is possible.

- Choose a few scenes or sequences from your favorite Scary Movies. See if you can identify the way in which elements from the Toolbox of Dread are used to make these scenes more effective.
- Write at least one scary scene or sequence that makes use of the various elements from the Toolbox of Dread.

5
PUTTING THEORY
INTO PRACTICE

The cave you fear to enter holds the treasure you seek.
Joseph Campbell

Inevitably, many of the elements in the Toolbox of Dread refer back to the various concepts that we examined earlier in our broader exploration of the Sense of Dread. All of those ideas are available to you in developing your Premises, Concepts, Sequences, Scenes, and Beats.

Now let's see how it's done — or at any rate, how I've been applying these ideas in my own work.

I've chosen an example that was in development for a number of years, but which ultimately wasn't ever produced. There are always various reasons why movies get made and why they don't. This was a project that we developed with Charles Band at Full Moon Entertainment back around 2000, that went through a number of different variations. It turned out to be a bit too ambitious for Full Moon's budget range at the time and, for a while, we tried to develop it with an outside producing partner, but in the end, it just didn't happen.

Over the course of its development, as is often the case, it went through a number of title changes and revisions, as well as various changes from its treatment stage to the final script.

This version was fairly early in the development process.

HORRORVISION.COM TREATMENT

We open in a dank squatter's apartment in a basement somewhere, decorated with icons of motion picture and real-life monsters, posters of the Wolfman, newspaper clippings of real-life serial killers, blow-ups of bloody accident scenes and war atrocities. In the midst of the nastiness is a young woman, ANGEL BRIGGS, wired, anorexic, sitting at a computer terminal. She's typing, watching the screen with hypnotic intensity, breathing fast. She finishes typing and hits "enter."

The screen abruptly seems to dissolve into random flickers of color. Then, as Angel watches, something odd seems to happen. The surface of the screen seems to fall away, becoming a tunnel that plunges to infinity. She reaches a hand out toward the screen that no longer really seems to be there. But something else seems to be *reaching out* at the same time, stretching out from the depths of the monitor. It reaches out toward her, a thing vaguely like a hand, but almost transparent, as if made from glass. She reaches out to touch it, fingertip to fingertip. Abruptly, the glassy fingers elongate hideously, becoming things like tentacles, whipping around her outstretched arm, her torso, her throat. A single finger tentacle, its tip now sharp as a glass shard, plunges straight toward her eye. . . .

A few horrifying elements are introduced here in this opening scene. First, the dissolution/penetration of the monitor screen. This will be a running theme in the story and has been used in

various forms in a number of different movies, ranging from Tobe
Hooper's *Poltergeist* (1982) to David Cronenberg's *Videodrome*
(1983) to Hideo Nakata's *Ringu* (1998). Likewise, the innate fear
of having the eye damaged or penetrated.

> Later, we meet a tough, working-class woman
> Police Detective, LIEUTENANT EMMA BRADLEY, and
> her partner, JOHNNY BARNES. They're visiting
> the scene of Angel's death. The apartment is
> a scene of incredible slaughter. Angel was
> skinned—and there's no sign of the skin.

Again, the notion of a person being skinned — being reduced
to mere flesh — is intrinsically horrifying. And, of course, blood
and gore itself, produces a shocking reaction. Also, in the finished
script, the body is found in the bathtub; thus, the uneasy contrast
between the expected nakedness/intimacy of "nudity" in a bathtub, and the ultimate nudity of someone devoid of skin.

> Yet there seems to be no sign of anyone having
> been there other than the victim. In fact, the
> door appears to have been padlocked from the
> inside, and no other way for anyone to get in
> or out.
>
> Pursuing the investigation, the computer, cov-
> ered in blood and other unpleasant substances,
> is transported to the Department's computer
> expert, a droll, overweight character named
> DRISCOLL.
>
> Investigating the computer, he finds that there's
> a complex program that's been downloaded from a
> mysterious website—horrorvision.com. He can't
> say exactly what the program does, only that

it's a series of graphic and text puzzles, all
relating to aspects of human horror. But the
program also appears to be interactive in a way
that he's never seen before. The act of solv-
ing the puzzles, of moving through the program,
changes it, reconstructs the program.

And what's the final form of the reconstruc-
tion? No way to tell -- until you work your way
through it. Suspecting a connection between
the horror website and Angel's horrific death,
she tells Driscoll to work his way through the
program and find out just what it's supposed to
do.

Curious herself, Bradley taps into the website
on her own computer at home. Soon, she too is
working her way through the program, the same
way that Driscoll is.

Following up other clues, Bradley and Barnes
locate a pair of other Horrorvision "users."
They pay a visit to a black guy, JONAS SCOTT,
who manages a "Discovery Zone" type kid-play
place and explores the Horrorvision landscape
from a computer terminal tucked away in a back
room.

Here, in the final script, I looked to create a sense of unease
between the horrifying and graphic images being depicted on
Jonas' Horrorvision screen and the innocent children at play, visible on the other side of a two-way mirror in his office area.

He admits to knowing Angel. Both of them,
apparently, were mutually involved in their
cyberspace exploration of the Horrorvision
site. They, like Driscoll, were trying to work

their way through the program. Angel apparently succeeded. "And that's why she was killed?" Bradley asks. It doesn't make much sense. What exactly is the point of the Horrorvision site? What happens when you work your way through the program? What is it? What's the point of it? And why would anybody commit murder over it?

Jonas, who seems, if anything, enthusiastic about Angel's dramatic dissolution, tries to explain. Somebody—and no one knows who—created the Horrorvision site.

But it's more than simply a storehouse. It was designed as a program that would SEEK OUT horror on the web. In order to do that, the creator invented a program, using a new mathematical language that allows human concepts like love, hate, and fear, to be reduced to equations. The unknown programmer invented a "horror paradigm." Anything that matched the paradigm was copied into the Horrorvision program. Clearly, the program went looking in all sorts of places, some of which, perhaps, it shouldn't have gone. Now who knows what's inside? The only way to find out is to look. Jonas is looking.

When Jonas finds out that Bradley herself is investigating the site, he gives her a shortcut—a way to jump ahead in the program. Otherwise, she'll be wandering around inside it for months. Bradley gives the shortcut to Driscoll.

Later, the two cops pay a visit to another friend of Angel's—JEANETTE MEKAS, a Computer Nerd who lives alone in her apartment with her pet snake.

But when they come calling it appears as if Jeanette's missing something crucial for a computer nerd—a computer. It's clear that Jeannette has recently emptied her apartment—it looks as if she just moved in. It's also clear that she's terrified. They try to find out why. Who is trying to kill them? What's the motive?

But when she answers, she doesn't talk about killers and motives. She talks about the web. Only, she says, it isn't really a web. It's more like a growth medium, like the primordial seas. Things are born in it, grow in it, reproduce, die, evolve. Monitors and keyboards aren't input and output devices. They're shorelines, the shores of the cybernetic ocean.

People are myopic. Everybody talks about trying to get INTO cyberspace—to dive into the ocean. What people don't realize is that it's a two-way street. Just as we're trying to get in, there may be things INSIDE that are trying to break out.

Just as sea life first colonized dry land, maybe there are things in the cybersea that are doing their best to cross the shoreline, to colonize dry land—OUR world.

Needless to say, Barnes thinks that Jeanette is a few chips short of a cookie. Bradley, meanwhile, is interested in uncovering the creator of the website, whoever or wherever he is. There are hints that Jeanette might know, but she seems afraid to tell.

Later, Jeanette receives a mysterious telephone call. Instead of a voice, she hears the whine of a fax signal trying to get through.

But there's something else in the signal—perhaps the sound of screaming. The call prompts Jeanette to call up Bradley's number and leave a message. As she finishes, there's a knock at her door.

She looks through the peep hole and sees Angel on the other side. She doesn't know what to think. Paralyzed, she stares through the hole. Angel, silent, stares back, stares with one eye in particular. Abruptly, a thing like a shard of glass comes shooting out, through the peep hole, impaling Jeanette. In a moment, a thing that seems halfway between gelatin and glass has literally poured out of Angel's skin and come through the door....

Later. Jeanette's death is as mysterious as the first. Barnes wonders if they should contact the F.B.I. Everything seems to suggest a serial killer using the Web to identify potential victims. But Bradley wants to hold off. She isn't sure about a serial killer, although she has no clear alternative. She's a Detective who believes that the only way to solve a case is to go where the evidence takes you. Wherever it goes.

Through Jeanette's cryptic telephone message, they manage to track down the initial location of the Horrorvision site—it's coming by way of a satellite link-up from an isolated little desert town named Grazey. Bradley and Barnes make plans to head out there the following day.

It was clear as I moved to script that two things were missing in this initial treatment. First, while there are always going to be things left out of a treatment, there were no real details about the Horrorvision Website itself and that, especially, would need to be developed. Second, and more critically, there was very little development in Bradley's character (who I would later rename "Wright" — because it's always a mistake to have two main characters whose names start with the same letter). She was the central character, our Protagonist, and Protagonists need a "central tension," an internal conflict that relates to the story's theme and that's going to be developed and explored over the course of the story. And Bradley really didn't have one. She and Barnes weren't very different as characters in this initial pass.

In remedying the former situation, I created a creepy "host" to the Website in the form of "Pig Girl" — a Pig with a Pretty Girl's face, thus giving the environment a kind of diabolical personality, allowing users to converse with it.

As for Bradley/Wright, I realized that, for her to connect to the larger story, she needed to be drawn to the website, in her own way, very much as the earlier victims had been drawn, as opposed to simply doing it as part of her job. Thus, I introduced the notion that the special shortcut that got you close to the end of the program required that you had to have experienced real horror in your own life.

Thus, I gave her such an experience, which she has to confess to the "Pig Girl" at one point in the story, detailing the death of her child, who choked to death on a Christmas ornament — on a little Baby Jesus. The story actually gets much worse from there, bringing her face to face not only with grief and loss, but also with her own darkest impulses. Suffice it to say, she gets the "virtual key" that leads her close to the end of the program.

Shortly after making this shocking confession and receiving the "key" that will potentially lead her close to the end of the program

— to the revelation of the "horror paradigm" — the following scene takes place.

But from this point on, Bradley/Wright is not only a potential victim of the Horrorvision Program. Having experienced true horror herself, she finds herself drawn to it — and at the same time is repelled by it, wanting not only to destroy it but to destroy the impulse it embodies within herself.

```
But that night, Bradley hears a knock at HER
door. She looks out through her peep hole.
Nobody appears to be there. But the knocking
continues. When she shouts, there's no answer.
She draws her gun and opens the door. At first,
there appears to be nobody there. Then she
looks back toward the door. A disembodied human
hand is clinging there, but instead of ending
in the stump of a wrist, the thick tail of a
snake has somehow been grafted to it, forming
a kind of bizarre chimerical creature.
```

A few horrifying elements here. First, the notion of a "chimera," an unnatural combination, especially of something human and something from the animal kingdom, creates a distinct sense of unease. Second, of course, anything related to snakes presses our innate fear of serpents. Finally, the "softness" beneath the apparently solid body of the creature, indicating that the thing is, after all, a mere skin on top of something without real form, is likewise intended to add another layer of horror to the proceedings.

```
The thing leaps off the door and grabs for
Bradley. There follows a nightmarish battle.
The thing appears, as with Angel, to be lit-
tle more than a skin holding some unpleasantly
alive gelatin. Ultimately, Bradley discovers
```

that the stuff, whatever it is, can burn and
uses the fire from the gas range to destroy it.

*Please note that following the Treatment, the Scene in Grazey
will be presented in full, excerpted from the finished screenplay.

On their way out to the desert, Bradley tries
to tell Barnes about what happened, but it's
clear that he's shutting this off. He doesn't
even WANT to know.

They reach Grazey, which is just a scattered
collection of mobile homes out in the middle
of nowhere. It isn't hard to figure out the one
they're interested in—it's the one with the
big antenna dish out in front. It also has a
man out in front, BARON MUSCOFF, ragged, awkwardly shaped, wearing cheap, ill-fitting work
clothes, doing his best to keep a motley collection of weeds alive with a garden hose. They
ask to see him inside. He calmly agrees.

The inside of his mobile home is a nightmare.
Like the basement in the first scene, it's a
collection of horrors, memorabilia of death
and corruption. The house stinks of decay and
is infested with flies. Muscoff doesn't seem to
mind, doesn't even act as if it's out of the
ordinary. When they question him about Angel and
Jeanette he calmly shows them their rolled-up
skins—and the skins of others, apparently gotten in the same way. The two may have noticed
that the town is rather quiet. That's to be
expected. He's the only one left.

Barnes is now sure that they've caught their
serial killer, but Bradley knows better. She
realizes that something hideous and impossible

is going on. She questions the composed Muscoff. What is the paradigm for Horror? What is it that the program searched for? Muscoff tries to explain. What do ghosts and concentration camps and serial killers and werewolves and mothers who roast their babies in ovens all have in common? Not death. Not even violence.

Horror is about the sudden penetration of barriers that we think of as impermeable. The barrier between human and beast, between life and death, between good and evil, between soul and flesh. We think that unbreakable walls separate those things, but in fact, the barriers are just smoke. And that smoke is the place where Horror dwells.

Bradley asks, what about the barrier between the world inside the computer, the world of ones and zeros, and the REAL world, outside. Is that one of his "impermeable" barriers?

Of course, Muscoff answers. And if the Horrorvision program were to find, by some chance, an experimental program designed to breach that barrier, it would identify it as such, and absorb it into its matrix.

Then all it would take would be for somebody—anybody—to execute the program and the wall between the cybernetic world and our own would simply slip away and the program would step out, into the real world.

And what would such a thing look like? What does a program look like when it steps out of the computer?

Muscoff answers that it would be amorphous,

at first. It would need other living things to provide templates for it to move about. Skins.

But it's an intelligent program. It learns about its new home, makes adjustments. And what one learns, it can teach to others. As more and more people complete the Horrorvision program, more and more of them will come through, to colonize.

Barnes, who thinks the whole thing is nuts, has had enough. He goes to handcuff Muscoff.

Bad mistake.

Muscoff is, of course, one of the things and in an instant, its gelatin-like tentacles are holding Barnes immobile. One of his fingers becomes a thing like a dagger of glass. It becomes clear that Muscoff intends to skin Barnes alive.

Bradley, who knows from the night before that gunfire is no use against these things, produces a coke-bottle Molotov cocktail with a lighter taped to the neck. One flick of her thumb will ignite it.

It poses an interesting problem. The being clearly has no experience with Mexican stand-offs. But, unnoticed by Bradley, a solution appears to be resolving behind her.

The flies, buzzing so busily in the air, begin to drop to the floor, one by one.

They, like Muscoff are, in fact, only hollow shells, each holding a tiny speck of one of the computer organisms. As they fall to the floor, unseen behind her, the gelatin of which the organisms are made begins to flow out of the fallen flies and recombine.

At the last instant, Barnes spots it and shouts a warning as the Thing, like a translucent bat, comes springing through the air like a cannon shot. Instinctively, Bradley hits the lighter switch and flings the bottle. It hits the flying Thing in mid-air. It bursts into flame.

Bradley ducks as it goes flying across the air toward Muscoff and Barnes. Muscoff shoves Barnes toward the burning Thing and ducks. The Thing, still burning, hits Barnes with a thud, knocking him to the ground. Its momentum carries it to the far side of the mobile home.

As it hits the floor it seems to unfold, spreading fire everywhere. As the fire begins to flow back toward the stunned Barnes, Bradley grabs him and hauls him out of the mobile home. She can see Muscoff, the human skin burning off of him, being consumed by the fire.

In a matter of moments, the mobile home is gone, burned up. But not the threat. The source of the horror website has been destroyed. It's off the net. But at least two people have downloaded the Horrorvision program. Jonas—and Driscoll.

They head back to town. Bradley radios ahead and tries to get in touch with Driscoll, but he doesn't seem to be at his desk and nobody seems able to find him.

She tells his assistant to destroy Angel's computer. Wreck it. Burn it. Leave no retrievable data behind. And every other hard drive or disk she can find in Driscoll's office as well. Everything. Every bit of data in his office has to be destroyed.

Meanwhile, Bradley and Barnes go looking for Jonas. If Bradley's right, he won't be at home. He'll be at the Discovery Zone, now after hours, exploring his copy of the Horrorvision program.

Jonas is, in fact, in his little back room, rapidly approaching the conclusion of the Horrorvision program. Bradley and Barnes arrive at the critical juncture. But Jonas has gone too far. He can't back out. He enters the final code and one of the Horrorvision beings comes pouring out of the monitor as if squeezed out of a toothpaste tube, tearing him to pieces.

There follows a desperate game of hunter and hunted, carried out in the darkened confines of the Discovery Zone.

Bradley has to hunt the gelatin-like organism, flare in hand, through the intricate network of a multileveled indoor playground complete with ball room, climbing nets and child-sized tunnels.

As matters become more desperate, Driscoll, now a skin inhabited by another of the Horrorvision organisms, appears.

In the finished screenplay, I establish that Driscoll has become one of "them" in two ways. First, his eyes turn to look at Barnes — one at a time — something that, obviously, no human eyes are capable of doing. A small but disturbingly inhuman action. Second, when Barnes pulls away from him, moving behind a clear Plexiglas wall, Driscoll slips and his face falls against it, at which point his mouth, nose, cheeks, forehead, all go completely flat against the transparent surface — confirming that there's nothing solid behind Driscoll's skin.

```
Ultimately, both of the Horrorvision organisms
are destroyed, but Barnes dies in the process.
Bradley escapes alone and the fire that inev-
itably follows, destroys any evidence of the
organisms' existence.

It's okay with Bradley. She wouldn't know how
to write a report about something so unlikely.
She wants to get back to her normal life, one
where all the walls are up. But when she returns
to her apartment, there's an unpleasant sur-
prise waiting on her computer. The Horrorvision
program is still there. It's not on her hard
drive. It's still coming in from over the web.
It still exists, somewhere out in cyberspace.
As we MOVE AWAY from her, we can see the site
as unwary users tune it in all across the coun-
try, in offices, in homes—everywhere.
```

• • •

What follows is the sequence from the completed screenplay, starting with Bradley (now renamed Wright) and Barnes arriving at Grazey and finding Baron Muscoff.

```
EXT. THE HIGHWAY - DAY


Barnes and Wright are in the car, heading for
Grazey.
```

INT. THE CAR - DAY

Barnes is driving. Wright looks distinctly the
worse for wear.

>   WRIGHT
>   Look, I know how this sounds, believe
>   me. I mean, can you imagine me going
>   into the captain and telling him that
>   this thing that looks like a snake with
>   a hand...

>   BARNES
>   (distinctly uncomfortable)
>   Look, um, look -- Annie. You know
>   whatever the deal is, I'm going to back
>   you up but, the way I have to look
>   at it --

>   WRIGHT
>   Look, I know --

>   BARNES
>   Christ, just shut up and listen to me.
>   I'm telling you that what happened to
>   you was you being exhausted and getting
>   confused between what was real and what
>   was a dream. That's it. 'Cause I'm
>   thinking the only other alternative
>   is something along the lines of a
>   mental breakdown.

                    WRIGHT
        Johnny --

                    BARNES
        -- and then I'd have to take certain
        actions, in terms of filing a report,
        and about you being on active duty and
        carrying a weapon and what have you.
        And I am begging you not to force me
        into that position. Okay? So, let's
        just drop this thing.

Wright realizes the quandary that Barnes is in. She
softens.

                    WRIGHT
        Okay. Okay. I see what the problem is.
        Okay.
                    (pause)
        On the other hand, when we get where
        we're going, I think that you have to
        go into this with an open mind.

Wright manipulates something that she's concealing
under her jacket. We hear a clink like glass
against glass.

                    WRIGHT
        I know *I* am.

Barnes looks at her, worried and unhappy.

It shouldn't be much of a surprise even without having read the treatment, that Wright has brought along some Molotov cocktails which is given away here by the glass "clink" under her jacket. But that raises another question, which is just why it is that the Horrorvision organisms are so vulnerable to fire, a question unaddressed in the treatment.

On a strictly practical level, I needed the Horrorvision organisms to have some sort of vulnerability or there couldn't be any sort of dramatic action in the scenes where our protagonists confront them. Ideally, in any such confrontation between opposing forces, you want the protagonists to be overmatched (at least until the end, if then), but not totally overmatched or "the end" will happen at the very first confrontation. Antagonists need to be powerful, but not invulnerable.

So the question remains — why fire, in particular? The answer *within the story* can't simply be "because otherwise there wouldn't be a story." There should be an answer that makes sense within the realm of the narrative itself — so later on, within this scene, I do attempt to come up with some rationale for the Horrorvision organisms' vulnerability to fire.

EXT. GRAZEY, ARIZONA - DAY

This is a small collection of mobile homes plunked down in the middle of absolutely nowhere for absolutely no reason.

There's a crude water tower, a gas station, a diner, and no sign of a living soul. The car pulls up and comes to a stop.

Wright and Barnes come out of the car, Wright still
wearing her jacket.

                    BARNES
         Aren't you hot in that thing?

                    WRIGHT
         I'm comfortable.

Barnes goes to the garage adjoining the gas
station. He opens the door.

                    BARNES
         Hello? Hello, in there?

He steps in. Wright looks around. Nothing. Nobody.
A few seconds later, Barnes emerges.

                    BARNES
         Nobody in there.

                    WRIGHT
         Nobody seems to have bothered putting
         house numbers on any of these things.

                    BARNES
         What's the point? There probably aren't
         more than thirty or forty people in the
         whole town. Let's ask at the diner.

They head across the dusty street to the diner.

It's dark inside, the door a pit of darkness
against the bright outside. Barnes pushes his way
in. Wright follows.

INT. THE DINER - DAY

Like the gas station, it's open, but empty. No
customers. Nobody behind the counter.

                    BARNES
        Hello? Hello there?

Wright goes to the counter and steps behind it. She
checks the grill.

                    WRIGHT
        The grill is cold.

She's about to step out when she sees something
down on the floor.

                    WRIGHT
        Johnny.

Sensing the alarm in her voice, Barnes is there in
an instant. She gestures down to the floor. There's
a huge brown stain there, covering the floor,
splattering up onto the tiles and the inside of the
counter.

```
                    BARNES
        Blood?

She takes up a bit of the dried stuff and examines
it on a fingertip.

                    WRIGHT
        I think so.

                    BARNES
        I'll check the kitchen.

He pushes the kitchen door open and looks inside.

                    BARNES
        Annie.

Wright moves to the door and looks over his
shoulder.

INT. KITCHEN - DAY

The tiny kitchen is spattered all over with blood,
now dried to an ugly brown like the other stain.
```

From the time that Wright and Barnes come out onto the main street of Grazey, I begin to ratchet the tension, at first not by what they see and hear but by what they don't. It's a town without people, without sound or movement. As they move deeper into it, the indications of violence continue to grow — the tension continues to ratchet.

EXT. THE TOWN - DAY

Wright, gun drawn, is hammering on the door to one
of the mobile homes. Barnes comes out of the home
next door.

                    BARNES
        Nobody. And blood in there, too. Jesus
        Christ, what's going on here?

                    WRIGHT
        Just hold on.

She hammers again, hesitates, then kicks in the
flimsy door. She steps inside.

INT. THE MOBILE HOME - DAY

Nobody there. It's cluttered with the shabby
remains of somebody's life. Wright looks left and
right.

                    WRIGHT
        Hello? Hello?

She looks at an unfolded bed, soaked with dried
blood. She turns. Nearby, is an empty crib,
similarly spattered. Her face grim, she steps back
out.

Drawing on intimate locations here: the bedroom and the bed stained with blood — and ratcheting again — to the blood-spattered crib, with the implication of a dire end to its occupant.

```
EXT. THE TOWN - DAY


She backs out. Barnes is looking pale.


                    BARNES
          It's the same everywhere. It's the
          whole goddam town, isn't it? They're
          all gone. I mean, tell me something
          else that makes sense. I mean, if this
          makes any fucking sense--


                    WRIGHT
               (hearing something)
          Quiet.


                    BARNES
          Look, we've got to --


                    WRIGHT
               (more insistent)
          Shhh!


Barnes freezes, listens, gun at the ready. Wright
is listening hard, too. But what they're hearing is
deceptively commonplace -- the splash of water.
```

The goal here is to continue the ratcheting, not with something dire, but with something both mundane and at the same time out of place, in this case, the sound of splashing water in the midst of this dry desert town.

                    WRIGHT
          Johnny, I need you to promise me
          something.

                    BARNES
          Like what?

                    WRIGHT
           Give me some slack. Let me handle it.

                    BARNES
          Annie --

                    WRIGHT
          If you don't believe anything, believe
          this. This is my territory. Just give
          me some slack.

                    BARNES
          I'll give you what I can.

Wright draws her weapon, gestures to Barnes to
follow. They circle around, behind the row of
mobile homes.

A big mobile antenna dish, some fifteen feet across, aimed at the sky, dominates one of the mobile homes at the far end of the row. They move cautiously toward it.

EXT. MUSCOFF'S MOBILE HOME - DAY

The two Detectives move around the big dish of Muscoff's antenna. His mobile home comes into view. A shabby little garden has been planted at the front of his mobile home.

MUSCOFF is standing in the garden, watering it with a garden hose. He's late middle-aged, ragged, awkwardly shaped, wearing cheap, ill-fitting work clothes. He doesn't seem at all alarmed when the two Detectives, weapons at the ready, approach him.

> WRIGHT
> Baron Muscoff?

> MUSCOFF
> Uh huh.

His perfectly inoffensive response is off-putting. Wright hesitates.

> WRIGHT
> Um -- we'd like to ask you a few questions.

Barnes looks at her. Clearly, she's already in need
of "slack."

                    MUSCOFF
        Go ahead.

                    WRIGHT
        Can we go inside?

                    MUSCOFF
        Sure. Why not?

He turns off the hose, goes to the door and opens
it. He gestures for Wright to enter.

Weapon at the ready, she steps inside.

Muscoff gestures for Barnes to follow. Barnes waves
Muscoff in with his gun. Muscoff shrugs and moves
in.

Barnes, aiming his weapon at Muscoff's back,
follows.

Here, again, the meeting with Baron Muscoff, his "shapeless" form,
his mild, bland affect, even what he's doing — watering his little
garden — and his equally bland responses to their questions, all
serve to amplify the tension of the situation, to continue tighten-
ing the spring. Readers know that something nasty is coming, but
the longer they have to wait, the greater the tension.

INT. MUSCOFF'S MOBILE HOME - DAY

Wright is standing a few steps inside the door,
holding her hand against the smell. Her eyes are
wide.

The air is filled with the sound of buzzing flies and
the tiny forms are visible, flitting through the
air.

Muscoff comes up behind her, with Barnes a step
behind. Barnes winces at the smell, covers his
nose.

                    MUSCOFF
          How do you like it?

Wright moves away from Muscoff, further into the
mobile home.

Note that, apart from the buzzing of the flies, which foreshadows what the mobile home contains, both Wright and Barnes see and react to the contents of Muscoff's home before it's shown/described.

The inside of his mobile home is a nightmare. Like
the basement in the first scene, it's a collection
of horrors, memorabilia of death and corruption.

This refers back to Angel Briggs' basement apartment.

A network of interlinked computers peeks out from
the midst of the collected horrors. Muscoff moves
into the midst of his home and tugs a couple of
chairs out.

Barnes meanwhile, is clutching his weapon in
both hands, aiming it straight at Muscoff's
heart. Muscoff, for his part, doesn't seem at all
perturbed, either by the flies, the smell, the
horrors, or the two Detectives.

> MUSCOFF
> Have a seat?

Neither Detective budges.

> WRIGHT
> No thank you.

> MUSCOFF
> What can I do for you?

> WRIGHT
> Is this where HORROR comes from? I mean
> the -- the website. Is this where it
> comes from? Is it yours?

Please note, at this point, the screenplay, as well as the name of the
website, had been changed from Horrorvision.com to H-rr-r.com
— which was, of course, simply pronounced "Horror." As often

happened with these projects, they went through a number of title changes during development.

>   MUSCOFF
>   Well, this is where it comes from. I
>   don't know that it's really, truly mine
>   anymore. Or anybody's. Can I get you
>   something to drink?

>   WRIGHT
>   No, thank you.

>   MUSCOFF
>   (to Barnes)
>   You?

Barnes, still pointing the gun at Muscoff's chest, shakes his head no.

>   BARNES
>   No. Annie--

>   WRIGHT
>   Mr. Muscoff, we're investigating the
>   murder of Angel Briggs and Jeanette
>   Mekas. Do you know anything about it?

>   MUSCOFF
>   Oh, sure. Hold on a sec.

He goes to a chest of drawers and pulls it open.
Barnes steps forward, ready to shoot.

                    BARNES
          Uh uh!

Muscoff hesitates.

                    WRIGHT
          Please, Mr. Muscoff, we need you to
          keep your hands in sight.

                    MUSCOFF
          Well, you asked. What if I just do it
          real slow? Hmm?

He moves his hand slowly into the drawer and
tugs out what appears, at first, to be some sort
of garment. But as it comes all the way out, it
becomes clear that it's a human skin. He looks at
it.

                    MUSCOFF (cont'd)
          I think this is -- no, this isn't her.
          Hold on.

He drops the skin on the floor. We can see the face
of some girl we haven't seen before, the eyes still
set in the face but her skin otherwise empty. He
tugs the drawer all the way open.

A swarm of flies come buzzing out.

There are other skins inside, folded like shirts.
He begins going through them, shoving them over,
tugging some out and dropping them.

> MUSCOFF (cont'd)
> No, that's not even a woman. Just --
> okay. Here's Angel.

He tosses one of the skins onto the floor near them.

> MUSCOFF (cont'd)
> Now, where's Jeanette? Where's
> Jeanette? Where's Jeanette?

He begins searching through other drawers. Flies
come swarming.

All the drawers are filled with human skins, some
men, some women, some old, some young.

Obviously, it's not simply the presence of the human skins that inspires horror, though of course it does, but the casual way in which Muscoff has stored them, folding and stowing them like so many garments in drawers, and as we see later, hanging them on hangers. Once again, we look for that collision between the normal/conventional and the abnormal to intensify the sense of dread.

Needless to say, the flies also add to our sense of unease.

                    MUSCOFF (cont'd)
I should take better care of these.
I guess you noticed that the town's
pretty quiet.

                    WRIGHT
We noticed.

                    MUSCOFF
That makes sense, really. Nobody's
left. Well, sort of. Do me a favor.
Check those closets behind you.

Barnes hesitates, then slides open one of the
closets.

Human skins hang there in neat rows. He reaches out
to touch them, can't quite bring himself to. He
goes to the next closet and slides that one open.

There's only one thing hanging there, and while
human skins appear to have been the raw material,
it looks anything but human, an aggregate of sewn-
together limbs knitted into something utterly
inhuman.

Barnes lifts it out by the hangar and studies it.

Muscoff notices.

> MUSCOFF (cont'd)
> Oh, yeah. That one. I guess we were
> getting a little creative there.

Barnes turns the thing, sees rows of eyes knitted
into the flesh of the thing -- eyes of different
colors.

Here we're obviously setting up a new, additional element that
wasn't present in the treatment — the chimerical being created
by sewing together multiple human limbs — a sort of spider-like
human form, seen here, at first, as simply a "skin."

He drops the thing to the floor, gets Muscoff back
in the site of his gun.

> MUSCOFF (cont'd)
> Oh, here's Jeanette. Too bad she's
> short a hand.

He tosses Jeanette's skin on the floor. There's the
bald head, the ring still through her nose.

One of her hands is missing -- the one used in the
ill-fated snake chimera the night before.

> BARNES
> Annie? How the fuck much slack do you
> need?

                    WRIGHT
Just hold on.

                    BARNES
Annie, what are we doing here?

                    WRIGHT
Just -- just shut up, all right? Just
stand there and shut up.

Muscoff stands, watching and listening, utterly
unperturbed. Wright turns to him.

                 WRIGHT (cont'd)
Mr. Muscoff, what is it that your
program searched for? The Horror
algorithm?

                    MUSCOFF
You already have the answer, really.
You had it last night.

                    WRIGHT
Tell me.

                    MUSCOFF
It's clearer when it's expressed
mathematically. It's related to
impermeable barriers. The barrier
between man and animal, life and death,

MUSCOFF (cont'd)

steel and flesh. But the fact is, those
barriers are just smoke. That smoke --
that smoke is the place where Horror
lives.

Wright is thinking now, trying to put things
together.

WRIGHT

And what about -- what about the
barrier between the world inside the
computer and the REAL world, outside.
Is that one of your "impermeable"
barriers?

MUSCOFF

Yes, you understand. Every generation
has its own magic, you see. These
programs, the hardware and the software
are this generation's spells and words
of power. Complete the ritual, reach
the end, and the program steps out,
into the real world.

BARNES

Christ, Annie --

WRIGHT

And what would a program look like when
it steps out of a computer?

                    MUSCOFF
Yes, well, at first it would be
amorphous. Sentient, but innocent. It
would need other living things to give
it form.

                    WRIGHT
Skins.

                    MUSCOFF
Yes. That way they can move around
without attracting attention. Learn
about the world. They're intelligent,
you know. What one learns, it can teach
to others.

                    WRIGHT
Others?

                    MUSCOFF
Of course. The longer the program is
around, the more people complete it,
more and more of—them -- will come
through, to colonize.

Muscoff starts to move toward Annie -- slowly,
not threatening, but coming close. Barnes has had
enough.

                    BARNES
     Stop! Now!

Muscoff stops, but now he's very close to Annie.

                    BARNES (cont'd)
     Annie --

                    WRIGHT
     Johnny.

                    BARNES
          (being "official")
     LIEUTENANT! I believe that we should
     handcuff this suspect and take him to
     the car. Now.

                    WRIGHT
     Dammit, Johnny, you don't know what
     we're in the middle of!

                    BARNES
     That's enough. I'm going to handcuff
     this motherfucker and take him to the
     car!

                    WRIGHT
     Johnny, stay away from him!

Barnes takes a step toward Muscoff, who shows no
sign of being disturbed by any of this.

> BARNES
> Face the wall, put your hands on your
> head.

Muscoff turns toward Barnes, impassive, staring at
him.

> WRIGHT
> Johnny, stay away from him!

Of course, we've known from Muscoff's first introduction that he was one of "them" — and that's part of the ratcheting tension that continues to play throughout the scene. That suspense is intensified by the fact that, while Wright understands this, Barnes obviously does not — and so that plays out as an additional element of concern for Wright.

Barnes takes another step forward and puts his gun
to Muscoff's head.

> BARNES
> I said, put your hands on top of your
> head.

Muscoff stares at Barnes, dispassionately.

Then, in an instant, he raises one hand and grabs
the arm that's holding the gun.

Barnes, tight as a wire to begin with, promptly
FIRES, point blank, against Muscoff's head.

The force of the impact shoves his head back, but he doesn't fall, doesn't let go of Barnes' hand.

Barnes, eyes wide with terror, stares at Muscoff, who now has a neat hole burnt into the middle of his forehead.

But no blood comes out. Instead, Barnes can see a glistening spot of transparent gelatin within the tiny disk of the bullet hole.

It pulses and moves slightly.

Barnes tries to pull away from Muscoff. He reaches up and grabs Muscoff's arm with his free hand.

His fingers sink into the soft material of Muscoff's arm.

Again, there is that unsettling element of something that we expect to be relatively hard — Muscoff's arm — yielding as if there were no bones in it as all, revealing itself to be composed of the gelatin-like material of the Horrorvision Organisms.

Abruptly, the gelatin flows out of the bullet hole like a snake, STRAIGHT TOWARD Barnes. Other tentacles emerge from his fingertips, wrapping around him.

In an instant, the tips of the tentacles solidify into gleaming transparent blades.

They make for Barnes' mouth, sliding in.

The mouth, especially the inside of the mouth is particularly sensitive — so the notion of multiple blades inside Barnes' mouth, as opposed to any other place that those blades might be poised to kill, is a choice intended to amplify the sense of horror.

                    BARNES (cont'd)
          Fuck!

                    WRIGHT
          Stop or you'll die!

Muscoff turns and looks toward Wright, still unconcerned. Then the tentacles stop their deadly advance.

Wright is holding out a coke-bottle Molotov cocktail with a plastic cigarette lighter taped to the neck.

Her thumb is on the lighter. One flick of the lighter will ignite the cloth wick.

                    WRIGHT (cont'd)
          You know what this is?

Muscoff doesn't answer.

                    WRIGHT (cont'd)
I flick this and you'll make a real
pretty flame.

                    MUSCOFF
If you throw it, then you'll burn him
alive along with me.

                    WRIGHT
If you kill him, then I'll have no
reason NOT to throw this. And I think
we both know just how flammable you are.

                    MUSCOFF
Yes, yes, we do. I don't exactly know
why that is. Perhaps the residual
effect of some earlier mythology
absorbed by the program. Purification by
fire. Well, it's still a problem, isn't
it?

That's the rationale for the Creatures' vulnerability to fire, such as
it is. Again, many of these elements tend to be arbitrary — why a
stake through the heart for vampires, or a silver bullet for werewolves? Ultimately, the more time one takes for such justifications, the more attention you end up drawing to the thinness of
the rationale.

Muscoff's eyes drift away from Wright, looking up
into the surrounding air. He is looking at the
FLIES, which continue to buzz and flit about.

Unnoticed by Wright or Barnes, the flies begin to
fall to the floor behind her.

We MOVE DOWN to the floor. As each fly twitches to
stillness, a tiny fleck of gelatin crawls out. They,
like Muscoff, are just hollow shells.

> MUSCOFF (cont'd)
> What to do. You want to live. I want to
> live.
> > (to Barnes)
> And I assume you want to live. But, at
> the same time, you need to kill me and
> I need to kill you.

> WRIGHT
> You know, people know where we are, why
> we came. If we die, they'll follow.
> Your little secret web site is done.

> MUSCOFF
> Yes, I think you're right.

DOWN ON THE FLOOR -- the flies continue to fall,
their liquid contents flowing underneath the
discarded "skin suit" that Wright dropped on the
floor.

Muscoff is clearly just talking to keep their
attention.

Abruptly, Barnes tries to pull free. The glass tentacles squeeze tighter -- the blades slip a little deeper inside his mouth.

> MUSCOFF (cont'd)
> I wouldn't do that if I were you, Detective.

Suddenly, a humped shape shambles up off the floor behind Wright. Barnes, unable to speak, gives a sharp cry.

Wright turns to face it. Her eyes go wide in terror.

The skin sack, now "filled," is a hideous thing, like a spider woven out of human limbs.

Of course, here I'm drawing on our instinctive horror of spiders, in this case a chimerical man-sized spider creature composed of human limbs and body parts. The shape of the thing was implied when the "skin" was first taken out of the closet and dropped on the floor. Now it's revealed here in all of its nightmarish glory.

It rears back and seems to spit. A ten-foot-long transparent razor-edged tongue SHOOTS OUT, directly at Wright. She ducks and the razor SKIMS HER SHOULDER.

She rolls down and hits the floor as the "tongue" draws back in. The Spider-thing starts forward and rears up again, ready to extrude its blade.

Wright screams, hits the lighter and FLINGS THE
BLAZING MOLOTOV COCKTAIL straight into the maw of
the Spider Thing.

It hits and bursts.

In an instant, the thing begins to burn like
napalm. It screams like the hand-snake and starts
flailing around, wildly.

It rushes toward Wright, who throws herself down.
It goes pirouetting over her, blind now, heading
straight for Muscoff.

Muscoff instinctively shoves Barnes forward,
against the flaming mass, and ducks to the side.
Barnes smashes against the flailing horror.

Barnes rebounds, howling, and hits the floor, his
clothes burning. He starts rolling back and forth
on the floor, trying to put out the fire.

The burning Spider Thing continues on its mindless,
destructive course. It smashes through the
computers, setting things alight left and right.

Muscoff, backed to a corner, abruptly looks
straight up and opens his mouth. The mass of liquid
of which he's made begins to flow upward, emptying
out of Muscoff's skin, heading toward a vent high
on the wall, leading to the outside world.

In such a cluttered and confined space, the fire itself is terrifying. It's obvious that, as the fire spreads, our heroes literally have only moments to live in such a deadly space.

Additionally, the way in which Muscoff empties himself out — with the gelatin-like Horrorvision Organism flowing up out of his open mouth, emptying his body out as it escapes — is intended to resemble a kind of "inverted vomit," triggering our natural revulsion.

Wright, seeing the thing escaping, plucks a second Molotov cocktail out of her jacket, hits the lighter and flings it across the room.

It hits the floor at Muscoff's feet.

The FLAMES BLOSSOM UPWARD. They sweep over the escaping thing. It begins to twist and writhe against the wall.

Its upper edge slides back down from the vent as it's swallowed by fire. The Spider Thing, its skin consumed, is losing its form, splattering, spreading fire everywhere.

Wright, stumbles forward, grabs the struggling Barnes and hauls him toward the door.

EXT. OUTSIDE MUSCOFF'S HOME - DAY

Wright helps the scorched Barnes out of the house. His clothing is still burning.

She throws him to the ground, flinging dirt on him.
He comes up on his knees, struggling, his mouth
bloody from Muscoff's "blades."

                    WRIGHT
        Are you all right? Can you walk?

Barnes struggles to get up. He gasps out something.

                    BARNES
    ...pane tain...

                    WRIGHT
        What? What?

He scrambles up to his feet.

                    BARNES
        Propane tank!

                    WRIGHT
    Shit!

The two scramble away from the blazing house.

Abruptly, the propane tank on the side of the
mobile home goes critical and BLOWS.

The house essentially disintegrates in an earth-
shaking explosion.

BURNING SMITHEREENS go flying up into the air,
RAINING DOWN on the two as they scramble toward the
car.

The scene continues briefly after this, with the burning fragments from the explosion setting the whole town on fire and coming to rest on the nearby water tower, which abruptly explodes dumping dozens of now-burning Horrorvision organisms on the street below. They scream and writhe as they burn.

THE DEVELOPMENT PROCESS

As I indicated at the beginning of this Chapter, we began to develop this project around the year 2000 — over 20 years ago. So, what happened to it? Well, obviously, it was never produced. There are many reasons why screenplays end up on the screen and many reasons why they don't. Sometimes those reasons are related to problems with the script and sometimes not.

While the final script was quite effective, there were a couple problems that ultimately prevented it from reaching the screen. First, Full Moon Entertainment, at the time we started developing this project, was working exclusively in the Direct-to-Video market, which was still reasonably profitable back in the year 2000. Even so, for a project to be financially successful given Full Moon's budget constraints, it needed limited locations, cast, effects, et al. And *Horrorvision.com*, as it continued to move through various drafts, kept getting bigger and bigger, until it was rather too big for a Full Moon budget.

At a certain point, we decided to try to take it out and find a production partner with an eye toward a theatrical release, at which point we ran into another obstacle.

It turned out that there was another movie in development in a similar vein called *Feardotcom* written by Moshe Diament and Josephine Coyle — dealing with a Detective investigating mysterious murders linked to a diabolical website.

While there were many differences between the two projects, *Feardotcom* had gotten to the market first, had already been acquired and was in development at Warner Brothers — and the two sounded similar enough in broad outline that it took the wind out of the sails of our project.

So, it never sold.

It's unfortunate, but this sort of thing happens a lot, and ultimately, all you can do is shrug and write another screenplay.

That being said, I think that the work still contains some very effective scenes and sequences that, I hope, have been instructive as far as the practical approaches to putting horror on the page.

EXERCISES ·

Apply what you've learned in the above Chapters, using the techniques of ratcheting, Learned and Instinctive fears, etc., to create several scenes that will fill the reader with the "Sense of Dread."

WHY HORROR?

We can easily forgive a child who is afraid of the dark; the
real tragedy of life is when men are afraid of the light.
Plato

For those of us who have always loved horror, this is a question
that we're often asked by those who simply "don't get it." Why go
out of your way to scare yourself? What's the point? Why horror?

More than that, there have always been people who think of
horror stories as quite literally unhealthy, as depraved — the suggestion of course, being that people who are drawn to horrifying
images and activities in literature or comic books or on the screen
will no doubt be inspired to copy such things in real life.

Does that ever happen? Certainly, on occasion. We can't pre-
tend that it doesn't. On the other hand, Charles Manson listened
to the Beatles and thought that they were telling him to start a race
war — which he tried to do by sending his followers out to commit some of the most heinous murders of the Twentieth Century.
But one can hardly blame that on the Beatles.

In the same token, those who create tales of Horror and Dread,
whether on the page or on the screen, have every intention of
inspiring fear, but no intention of inspiring imitation.

So, is the goal simply to create that emotion? To produce that
Sense of Dread?

Maybe we need to take a step back. Why do we tell stories of any kind? What purpose do they serve? One thing is clear. Human beings are the only story-telling animal on Earth. Other animals love, hate, grieve, nurture, create families, make war, sing, court one another, form pair bonds, communicate — but they don't tell stories. That is a uniquely human undertaking.

We tell stories as a way of understanding ourselves, discovering our place in the universe, a way of finding meaning. We find stories amongst our oldest writings, accounts of gods, monsters, and heroes.

But what of horror? How does that enter into our storytelling? Why don't our stories simply inspire and enlighten?

That's because fear has always been the place we go to learn.

We go to the places we fear not only to learn about the dark corners of the world, but to learn about the dark corners of ourselves, to learn about that which we fear to question.

Are those around us who and what they appear to be?

Are *we* who and what we appear to be?

Is the world itself what it appears to be?

Fear is the place we go to seek answers to these questions.

About what dwells in the shadows.

About the nature of our society, our sacred institutions, and the world.

About ourselves.

And what we learn is not always to our liking.

That's why the Horror Genre is the Cinema of Subversion — because it is constantly telling us that what we think of as most safe, most secure, most sacred, most to be trusted and relied upon, may at any time be taken away from us or revealed to be something other than what it appears to be.

Of all the various kinds of storytelling that have come down to us out of history, the Tale of Horror is the one that forces us to question the nature of our beliefs, of the World Around Us, of our Gods, and of Ourselves.

So, keep writing — but keep the lights on!

ACKNOWLEDGEMENTS

For as long as I can remember, I've been reading horror, watching it on television, and on the motion picture screen, so first I have to acknowledge those early influences: the novels and short stories, the TV shows, and the movies that I devoured during the sixties and seventies.

Thanks to Edgar Allan Poe, H. P. Lovecraft, William Hope Hodgson, M. R. James, and countless others genre writers of my youth.

Thanks to Rod Serling and *The Twilight Zone*, along with Richard Matheson and Charles Beaumont. Thanks to Joseph Stefano and *The Outer Limits*. Both shows populated my sleep with nightmares.

Thanks to the countless low-budget horror, science fiction, and monster movies produced by Allied Artists, A.I.P., and others and to all those who made them — movies like *It: The Terror from Beyond Space*, *Caltiki, the Immortal Monster*, *Kronos*, *Tarantula*, *Enemy from Space*, *Atomic Submarine*, and *Voodoo Island*.

Special thanks to Bert I. Gordon's collection of "giant" movies — *The Cyclops*, *Earth vs. The Spider*, *The Amazing Colossal Man*, *War of the Colossal Beast*, and *The Beginning of the End*.

Despite their obvious flaws, they all succeeded in both entrancing and terrifying countless ten-year-old boys — of which I was one.

Likewise, thanks to Inoshiro Honda and Toho Studios for all of the Kaiju movies released during the sixties.

As I grew older and reached out to more daring and subtler fare, I must acknowledge the genuine masterworks of Horror and Suspense and their makers — Erle C. Kenton's *Island of Lost Souls*, Alfred Hitchcock's *Psycho*, Val Lewton and the collection of subtle horrors that he produced in the forties, George Romero and his seminal *Dead* movies, Robert Wise's *The Haunting*, Jack Clayton and his version of *Turn of the Screw* — *The Innocents*.

Finally, I wish to acknowledge the modern voices in Horror Cinema, those who continue to expand the genre and bring new viewers into it:

Robert Eggers with his chilling premier feature, *The Witch*, and his equally effective follow-up, *The Lighthouse*.

Ari Aster with a likewise terrifying first outing in *Hereditary*, which he followed up with his controversial but still effective *Midsommar*.

Jordan Peele brought his own personal and uniquely chilling perspective to the horror genre in *Get Out* and later *Us*.

Jennifer Kent, an Australian director, brought us a genuinely terrifying viewing experience in *The Babadook*, and followed it up with *The Nightingale*, a wrenching historical drama that, while not officially a horror movie, nevertheless manages to terrify the viewer.

My thanks go out to all of the above and countless others, both the Living and the Dead, for your work and your continuing Inspiration.

I also wish to acknowledge those who have helped me professionally: Richard Rubinstein, Mitch Galin, and the late Tom Allen of Laurel Entertainment, Charlie Band of Full Moon Entertainment, David Greathouse, who we worked with for many years as a producing partner, and Bob Shaye of New Line Cinema.

Also from the David Lynch Graduate School of Cinematic Arts at Maharishi International University, I would like to thank Dorothy Rompalske for her continuing support, as well as Matthew Kalil and Kathie Fong Yoneda, who encouraged me to write this book, and of course, the incomparable David Lynch, both a master of Dread and a unique genre unto himself.

SUGGESTED READING

BOOKS ADDRESSING THE PSYCHOLOGY OF FEAR

Animals in Translation, Temple Grandin and Catherine Johnson, 9780743247696, Simon & Schuster, Pub. Date: 2005

The Uncanny, Sigmund Freud, originally published in 1919 in German — currently in the public domain, this book is available on-line at: https://uncanny.la.utexas.edu/

BOOKS ON WRITING HORROR

Writers Workshop of Horror, Edited by Michael Knost, 0982493916, Horror Writers Association, Pub. Date: 2009

Stephen King's On Writing, Stephen King, 1439156816, Charles Scribner's Sons, Pub. Date: 2000

How to Write a Horror Movie, Neal Bell, 0367151650 Taylor and Francis Group. Pub. Date: April 2020

Horror Screenwriting: The Nature of Fear, Devin Watson 9781932907605, Michael Weise Productions. Pub date: 2009

The Scream Writer's Handbook: How to Write a Terrifying Screenplay in 10 Bloody Steps, Thomas Fenton 173355453X, Pub. Date: October 2018

FILMOGRAPHY

The Author acknowledges the copyright owners of the following motion pictures which were discussed or referenced in this book:

127 Hours. Directed by Danny Boyle. Los Angeles, California: Fox Searchlight, 2010. All Rights Reserved.

Alien. Directed by Ridley Scott. Los Angeles California: Twentieth Century-Fox Film Corporation, All Rights Reserved.

Aliens. Directed by James Cameron. Los Angeles, California: Twentieth Century-Fox Film Corporation, 1986. All Rights Reserved.

The Amazing Colossal Man. Directed by Bert I. Gordon. Los Angeles, California: American International Pictures, 1957. All Rights Reserved.

The Amityville Horror. Directed by Stuart Rosenberg. Los Angeles, California: American International Pictures, 1979. All Rights Reserved.

Apollo 13. Directed by Ron Howard. Burbank, California: Universal Pictures, 1995. All Rights Reserved.

Atomic Submarine. Directed by Spencer Gordon Bennet. Los Angeles, California: Allied Artists, 1959. All Rights Reserved.

The Babadook. Directed by Jennifer Kent. Adelaide, S. Australia, South Australian Film Corporation, 2014. All Rights Reserved.

The Bad Seed. Directed by Mervyn LeRoy. Burbank, California: Warner Brothers Pictures, 1956. All Rights Reserved.

The Beginning of the End. Directed by Bert I. Gordon. Los Angeles, California: Republic Pictures, 1957. All Rights Reserved.

The Birds. Directed by Alfred Hitchcock. Burbank, California: Universal Pictures, 1963. All Rights Reserved.

The Blair Witch Project. Directed by Eduárdo Sanchez and Daniel Myrick. Los Angeles, California: Artisan Entertainment, 1999. All Rights Reserved.

Blue Velvet. Directed by David Lynch. Wilmington, North Carolina: De Laurentiis Entertainment Group, 1986. All Rights Reserved.

Blood Vessel. Directed by Justin Dix. Detroit, Michigan: The Horror Collective, 2019. All Rights Reserved.

Bone Tomahawk. Directed by S. Craig Zahler. Silver Spring, Maryland: RJL Entertainment, 2015. All Rights Reserved.

Buried. Directed by Rodrigo Cortés. Paris, France: Kinology/ Studio 37, 2010. All Rights Reserved.

The Cabinet of Dr. Caligari. Directed by Robert Weine. Decla Bioscop AG, 1920. Released into Public Domain.

Caltiki, the Immortal Monster. Directed by Riccardo Freda and Mario Bava. 1960. All Rights Reserved.

Cape Fear. Directed by J. Lee Thompson. Los Angeles, California: Universal-International Pictures, 1962. All Rights Reserved.

Cape Fear. Directed by Martin Scorsese. Burbank, California: Universal Pictures, 1991. All Rights Reserved.

Cat People. Directed by Jacques Tourneur. Los Angeles, California: RKO Radio Pictures, 1942. All Rights Reserved.

The Cave. Directed by Bruce Hunt. Culver City, California: Screen Gems, 2005. All Rights Reserved.

Un Chien Andalou. Directed by Luis Buñuel. 1929. Released into the Public Domain.

Children of the Corn. Directed by Fritz Kiersch. Atlanta, Georgia: New World Pictures, 1987. 1984. All Rights Reserved.

Children of the Damned. Directed by Anton Leader. Beverly Hills, California: Metro-Goldwyn-Mayer, 1964. All Rights Reserved.

Chinatown. Directed by Roman Polanski. Universal City, California: A Paramount Penthouse Presentation, 1974. All Rights Reserved.

Close Encounters of the Third Kind. Directed by Steven Spielberg. Culver City, California: Columbia Pictures Corporation, 1977. All Rights Reserved.

The Conjuring. Directed by James Wan. New York City, New York: New Line Cinema, 2013. All Rights Reserved.

Creep. Directed by Christopher Smith, Santa Monica, California: Lions Gate Home Entertainment (U.S. Release), 2004. All Rights Reserved.

The Cyclops. Directed by Bert I. Gordon 1957. Los Angeles, California: Allied Artists Pictures, All Rights Reserved.

Dawn of the Dead. Directed by George Romero. New York City, New York: Laurel Entertainment, 1978. All Rights Reserved.

Day of the Dead. Directed by George Romero. New York City, New York: Laurel Entertainment, 1985. All Rights Reserved.

Death Line. Directed by Gary Sherman. Los Angeles, California: American International Pictures, (U.S. Distributor) 1972. All Rights Reserved.

Death Ship. Directed by Alvin Rakoff. Los Angeles, California: AVCO Embassy, 1980. All Rights Reserved.

Deep Blue Sea. Directed by Renny Harlin. Burbank, California: Warner Brothers, 1999. All Rights Reserved.

The Descent. Directed by Neil Marshall. Santa Monica, California: Lions Gate Films, 2006. All Rights Reserved.

The Desperate Hours. Directed by William Wyler. Universal City, California: Paramount Pictures, 1955. All Rights Reserved.

The Devil Times Five. Directed by Sean MacGregor and David Sheldon. New York City, New York: Cinemation Industries, 1974. All Rights Reserved.

Don't Be Afraid of the Dark. Directed by John Newland. New York City, New York: American Broadcasting Company, 1973. All Rights Reserved.

Don't be Afraid of the Dark. Directed by Troy Nixey. New York City, New York: Miramax Pictures, 2010. All Rights Reserved.

Don't Breathe. Directed by Fede Álvarez. Culver City, California: Screen Gems, 2016. All Rights Reserved.

Earth vs. The Spider. Directed by Bert I. Gordon. Los Angeles, California: Allies Artists Pictures, 1958. All Rights Reserved.

The End of the World. Directed by August Blom. 1916. Released into Public Domain.

Enemy from Space. Directed by Val Guest. Los Angeles, California: United Artists (U.S. Release), 1957. All Rights Reserved.

Event Horizon. Directed by Paul W. S. Anderson. Universal City, California: Paramount Pictures, 1997. All Rights Reserved.

The Evil Dead. Directed by Sam Raimi. New York City, New York, Renaissance Pictures, 1981. All Rights Reserved.

The Exorcist. Directed by William Friedkin. Burbank, California: Warner Brothers Pictures, 1973. All Rights Reserved.

The Exorcist Part II. Directed by John Boorman. Burbank, California: Warner Brothers Pictures, 1977. All Rights Reserved.

The Forest. Directed by Jason Zada. New York City, New York: Focus Features, 2016. All Rights Reserved.

Funny Games. Directed by Michael Haneke. U.S. Distributor: Attitude Films, 1997. All Rights Reserved.

Funny Games. Directed by Michael Haneke. Burbank, California: Warner Independent Pictures, 2007. All Rights Reserved.

Get Out. Directed by Jordan Peele. Burbank, California, Universal Pictures, 2017. All Rights Reserved.

Ghost Ship. Directed by Steve Beck. Burbank, California: Warner Brothers, 2002. All Rights Reserved.

Ghostwatch. Directed by Leslie Manning. Westminster, London, England: British Broadcasting Corporation, 1992. All Rights Reserved.

The Godfather. Directed by Francis Ford Coppola. Universal City, California: Paramount Pictures, 1974. All Rights Reserved.

Halloween. Directed by John Carpenter. Burbank, California: Universal Pictures, 1978. All Rights Reserved.

The Haunting. Directed by Robert Wise. Los Angeles, California: MGM/UA Entertainment, 1963. All Rights Reserved.

Hellraiser. Directed by Clive Barker. Atlanta, Georgia: New World Pictures, 1987. All Rights Reserved.

Hellraiser: Deader. Directed by Rick Bota. New York City, New York: Dimension Pictures, 2005. All Rights Reserved.

Henry: Portrait of a Serial Killer. Directed by John McNaughton. Philadelphia, Pennsylvania: MPI Home Video, 1986. All Rights Reserved.

Hereditary. Directed by Ari Aster. New York City, New York: A24, 2018. All Rights Reserved.

The Hills Have Eyes. Directed by Wes Craven. United States of America: Vanguard Releasing Group, 1977. All Rights Reserved.

The Host. Directed by Andrew Niccol 2013. Los Angeles, California: Open Road Films, All Rights Reserved.

The Innocents. Directed by Jack Clayton. Los Angeles, California: Twentieth Century Fox, 1961. All Rights Reserved.

Invasion of the Body Snatchers. Directed by Don Siegel. Los Angeles, California: Allied Artists, 1956. All Rights Reserved.

Island of Terror. Directed by Terence Fisher. Burbank, California: Universal Pictures, 1966. All Rights Reserved.

It Follows. Directed by David Robert Mitchell. New York City, New York: Radius TWC, 2014. All Rights Reserved.

It! The Terror from Beyond Space. Directed by Edward L. Cahn. Los Angeles, California: Allied Artists, 1958. All Rights Reserved.

Jaws. Directed by Stephen Spielberg. Burbank, California: Universal, 1975. All Rights Reserved.

Kronos. Directed by Kurt Neumann. Los Angeles, California: Twentieth Century-Fox Film Corporation, 1957. All Rights Reserved.

The Lighthouse. Directed by Robert Eggers. New York City, New York: A24, 2019.

The Manchurian Candidate. Directed by John Frankenheimer. Los Angeles, California: United Artists, 1962.

Marathon Man. Directed by John Schlesinger. Universal City, California: Paramount Pictures, 1976.

Midsommar. Directed by Ari Aster 2019. New York City, New York: A24,

Misery. Directed by Rob Reiner. Culver City, California: Columbia Pictures, 1990.

North by Northwest. Directed by Alfred Hitchcock. Beverly Hills, California: Metro-Goldwyn-Mayer, 1959.

Night of the Living Dead. Directed by George Romero. 1968.

The Nightingale. Directed by Jennifer Kent. New York City, New York: IFC Films, 2018.

The Omen. Directed by Richard Donner. Los Angeles, California: Twentieth Century-Fox Film Corporation, 1976.

Open Water. Directed by Chris Kentis. Santa Monica, California: Lions Gate Films, 2004.

The Others. Directed by Alejandro Amenábar. New York City, New York: Miramax Pictures, 2001.

Pandorum. Directed by Christian Alvart. Santa Monica, California: Summit Entertainment, 2009.

Panic Room. Directed by David Fincher. Culver City, California: Columbia Pictures Corporation, 2002.

Paranormal Activity. Directed by Oren Peli. Universal City, California: Paramount Pictures, 2007. All Rights Reserved.

Phantom of the Opera. Directed by Rupert Julian. Burbank, California: Universal Pictures, 1925. Released to the Public Domain.

Poltergeist. Directed by Tobe Hooper. Los Angeles California: MGM/UA Entertainment, 1982. All Rights Reserved.

Psycho. Directed by Alfred Hitchcock. Los Angeles California: Paramount Pictures, 1960. All Rights Reserved.

Planet of the Vampires. Directed by Mario Bava. Los Angeles, California: American International Pictures, 1965. All Rights Reserved.

Ringu. Directed by Hideo Nakata. Universal City, California: Paramount Pictures, 1998. All Rights Reserved.

Runaway Train. Directed by Andrei Konchalovsky. United States of America: Cannon Releasing, 1985. All Rights Reserved.

The Shining. Directed by Stanley Kubrick. Burbank, California: Warner Brothers, 1980. All Rights Reserved.

Stitches. Directed by Neal Marshall Stevens. Los Angeles, California: Full Moon Entertainment, 2001. All Rights Reserved.

The Strangers. Directed by Bryan Bertino. Universal City, California: Rogue Pictures, 2008. All Rights Reserved.

The Skeleton Key. Directed by Iain Softley. Burbank, California: Universal Studios, 2005. All Rights Reserved.

Straw Dogs. Directed by Sam Peckinpah. New York City, New York: ABC Motion Pictures, 1971. All Rights Reserved.

Svengali. Directed by Archie Mayo. Burbank, California: Warner Brothers (as the Vitaphone Company), 1931. All Rights Reserved.

Tarantula. Directed by Jack Arnold. Burbank, California: Universal Pictures, 1955. All Rights Reserved.

Texas Chainsaw Massacre. Directed by Toby Hooper. Memphis, Tennessee, Bryanston Distributing Company, 1974. All Rights Reserved.

The Thing from Another World. Directed by Christian Nyby. Los Angeles, California: RKO Radio Pictures 1951. All Rights Reserved.

The Thing. Directed by John Carpenter. Burbank, California: Universal Pictures, 1982. All Rights Reserved.

They Live. Directed by John Carpenter. Burbank, California: Universal Pictures, 1988. All Rights Reserved.

Thirteen Ghosts. Directed by Steve Beck. Burbank, California: Warner Brothers, 2001. All Rights Reserved.

Triangle. Directed by Christopher Smith. London England: UK Film Council, 2009. All Rights Reserved.

Underwater. Directed by William Eubank. Los Angeles, California: Twentieth Century Fox, 2020. All Rights Reserved.

Urban Legend. Directed by Jamie Blanks. Burbank, California: Tristar Pictures, 1998. All Rights Reserved.

Us. Directed by Jordan Peele. Burbank, California: Universal Pictures, 2019. All Rights Reserved.

Videodrome. Directed by David Cronenberg. Montreal, Canada: Telefilm Canada, 1983. All Rights Reserved.

Village of the Damned. Directed by Wolf Rilla. Beverly Hills, California: Metro-Goldwyn-Mayer, 1960. All Rights Reserved.

Voodoo Island. Directed by Reginald Le Borg. Los Angeles, California: United Artists, 1957. All Rights Reserved.

War of the Colossal Beast. Directed by Bert I. Gordon. Los Angeles, California: American International Pictures, 1958. All Rights Reserved.

When a Stranger Calls. Directed by Fred Walton. Culver City, California: Columbia Pictures Corporation, 1979. All Rights Reserved.

Who Can Kill a Child? Directed by Narcisco Serrador. Finivest/ Medusa Distribuzione: Penta Films, 1976. All Rights Reserved.

The Witch. Directed by Robert Eggers. New York City, New York: A24, 2015. All Rights Reserved.

Zombie. Directed by Lucio Fulci. West Hollywood, California: Blue Underground, 2004. All Rights Reserved.

ABOUT THE AUTHOR

 **Neal Marshall Stevens** has been a working professional in the entertainment industry for over thirty years. He began his career at Laurel Entertainment, where he wrote multiple episodes of the anthology series, *Monsters.* He worked as senior story editor for Laurel's productions of several mini-series (*Stephen King's The Stand, Stephen King's The Langoliers,* and *Stephen King's The Golden Years*), and made-for-TV movies (*Precious Victims, The Vernon Johns Story,* and several others). He then worked for Charles Band's Full Moon Entertainment, specializing in direct-to-video productions. Over the course of his association with Full Moon, he worked on over 50 produced motion pictures, including six entries in the popular *Puppetmaster* series.

He also wrote and directed the feature, *Stitches,* and worked with Charles Band to produce several recent web series, including *Trophy Heads* and *Ravenwolf Towers.*

Among other projects, Neal sold the original screenplay *Deader* to Dimension Pictures, which was subsequently produced as *Hellraiser: Deader,* and wrote the screenplay for Dark Castle's feature remake of *Thirteen Ghosts.*

In addition to his work as a screenwriter, Neal has taught online for eight years for Script University, and is currently an associate professor at the David Lynch Academy of Screenwriting at Maharishi International University.

ABOUT CHARLES BAND

Producer, director, mogul and renowned "B-movie" showman Charles Band has been the first name in low-budget, high-concept genre entertainment for over 40 years.

After forging an early career producing cult classics like *Tourist Trap* (one of Stephen King's favorite horror movies), *Mansion of the Doomed* (with Gloria Grahame and a young Lance Henricksen), and the 3D shocker *Parasite* (the first feature film to star Demi Moore), Band started his own studio, Empire Pictures. Through Empire, he produced, often directed, and distributed cult classics like *Re-Animator, Ghoulies, Trancers* (the first movie to star Helen Hunt), and *Troll*, while also acting as a pioneer in the home video market with his now iconic Meda (later renamed Media) Home Entertainment and Wizard Video labels.

Later, in 1989, Band created (aided by a distribution deal with Paramount Pictures) Full Moon Features, the juggernaut direct-to-video horror and fantasy studio that was responsible for the hugely successful *Puppet Master* franchise, *Subspecies, Cannibal Women in the Avocado Jungle of Death* (Bill Maher's first film), *Head of the Family, Pit and the Pendulum, Castle Freak* and hundreds of others.

Along the way, he invented a thriving merchandising empire, a popular streaming channel, multiple TV series, a line of clothing and toys, comic books, a popular film magazine, and much, much more.

MICHAEL WIESE PRODUCTIONS

I N A DARK TIME, a light bringer came along, leading the curious and the frustrated to clarity and empowerment. It took the well-guarded secrets out of the hands of the few and made them available to all. It spread a spirit of openness and creative freedom, and built a storehouse of knowledge dedicated to the betterment of the arts.

The essence of Michael Wiese Productions (MWP) is empowering people who have the burning desire to express themselves creatively. We help them realize their dreams by putting the tools in their hands. We demystify the sometimes secretive worlds of screenwriting, directing, acting, producing, film financing, and other media crafts.

By doing so, we hope to bring forth a realization of 'conscious media,' which we define as being positively charged, emphasizing hope, and affirming positive values like trust, cooperation, self-empowerment, freedom, and love. Grounded in the deep roots of myth, it aims to be healing both for those who make the art and those who encounter it. It hopes to be transformative for people, opening doors to new possibilities and pulling back veils to reveal hidden worlds.

MWP has built a storehouse of knowledge unequaled in the world, for no other publisher has so many titles on the media arts. Please visit www.mwp.com, where you will find many free resources and a 25% discount on our books. Sign up and become part of the wider creative community!

MICHAEL WIESE, Co-Publisher
GERALDINE OVERTON, Co-Publisher

CPSIA information can be obtained
at www.ICGtesting.com
Printed in the USA
JSHW030854021221
20871JS00001B/1

9 781615 933334